Not Just Another Colored Girl From The South

Not Just Another Colored Girl From The South

A MEMOIR

Mamie Ethel Thomas

ISBN: 0692546596
ISBN 13: 9780692546598
Printed by CreatespaceAvailable at Amazon.com, Barnes & Nobles, and
other retail outlets
Johnson-Thomas Publishing, Inc.
Made in the United States of America

Dedication

To the memory of Mama, Uncle Tom, and Aunt Esther
who recognized my potential and enabled me to become the
person I am today. To the legacy of my grandfather, "the good
man." I wish men everywhere would follow his example.

Acknowledgments

THANKS TO ROSIE SHEARD PARRIS, my classmate and sister-friend for her unwavering support.

Thanks to Terri Hall for being a good friend and trusted reader.

Special thanks to Dorette Saunders, my editor who has gone beyond the bounds of professional assistance. Thanks for the Bible verses

Contents

Contents

Introduction: Not Just Another Colored Girl From the South

⎯⎯ᴄ⎯⎯

Aʟᴛʜᴏᴜɢʜ I ᴡᴀs ɴᴇᴠᴇʀ ɢɪᴠᴇɴ details about my parents' relationship, I pieced together enough information to conclude that they had a "shot-gun wedding," because they only stayed together a few weeks or months, 'separated,' and never saw each other again. It was during the time of the Great Depression—a time when unemployment and poverty were equally rampant. I was abandoned soon after birth by my father and a few years later by my mother. I was raised in Emporia, Virginia, by my mother's mother and my mother's brother who lived near the Meherrin River. I remember how my grandmother used to say, "Things were so hard, I thought we would have to eat you."

The Great Depression which was caused by the stock market crash of 1929, ended in 1945 at the end of World War II. The federal government imposed rationing of staples like butter, sugar, gasoline, and other products. I vividly recall being allowed to open band-aid sized packets of yellow food coloring to mix with pound-sized blocks of lard to make it look and taste like butter.

The economy began to recover after the war ended and my grandmother and uncle opened a dancehall, Southern Club, and added a pool hall behind the existing barbershop where our old kitchen used to be. Soon afterwards, our house was converted into M.L. Weaver's Colored Tourist Home, catering to Colored musicians traveling the 'Chitlin' Circuit.'

My life took a drastic detour in my senior year of high school when my dream of becoming an opera singer vanished into thin air. It was too late to think about what might have been if our school had guidance counselors, senior advisors, or college recruiters who could have given guidance on resources such as scholarships, grants, and work-study programs. They would have informed me of my options as a student who was poised to excel. Instead, I was informed by my grandmother that although she could not afford to send me to college, she had devised a plan. She, my uncle and, most likely, his wife, decided that I should study nursing in New York City where my two aunts lived.

What did I know about nursing? I had never been in a hospital. There were no hospitals in Emporia, unless you considered Emporia's animal hospital. Soon family friends began to regale me with stories of hometown women who had left Emporia to become registered nurses. I was more than surprised to learn that a few of them were called Visiting Nurses. In some extraordinary circumstances some nurses, years later, served in the U.S. House of Representatives. These women include Karen Bass of California, Diane Black of Tennessee, Lois Capps of California, Renee Ellmers of North Carolina, Eddie Bernice Johnson of Texas, and Carolyn McCarthy of New York. Not knowing what the future held, I prepared to leave my family vowing to conquer every challenge that came my way.

I was among the "refugees" on the streets of Harlem, New York. I didn't realize, until many years later when I read Isabel Wilkerson's book *The Warmth of Other Suns* that I was part of the great migration of African Americans from the South to eastern and western states. I, too, had left my home for a better opportunity during the period 1915 and 1970. I had a great vantage point from my new home, Harlem Hospital's School of Nursing Residence, to observe many significant events in the lives of Blacks in Harlem. Sometimes I saw others, who like me had left the South, gathered at the corner of Lenox Avenue and 135th Street watching men who stood on an elevated platform, speaking loudly over a bullhorn. The men sounded a lot like Baptist preachers, but they were called 'Soap-Box Orators.' Nothing like this ever occurred in my hometown. I was somewhat amused and at the same time bewildered. Many of these men later became prominent civil rights leaders; one of whom was A. Phillip Randolph.

Somewhere along the way I discovered that migrating from the South to the North would not be my only journey. I developed a burning desire to travel to the Motherland and to countries where her children were scattered throughout the diaspora. Thankfully, I accomplished that goal. Even more important, I desired to escape the morass of segregation by reaching deep down to the well of resilience planted in me by my godly grandmother. Her values of faith, hope, education, and hard work opened doors of opportunities for my success and led me on the path to social activism. I am forever grateful to my grandfather, Walter H. Weaver, Sr., who laid a solid foundation and left a lasting legacy for our family. I have had a wonderful life.

CHAPTER 1

A Family of Entrepreneurs

"A good *man* leaves an inheritance to his children's children,
but the wealth of the sinner is stored up for the righteous."

PROVERBS 13:22, NKJV

IT ALL STARTED IN THE great state of Virginia with my grandparents, Walter Hamilton Weaver, Sr. and Mamie Louise Dickens Weaver of Emporia in Greensville County. My grandfather, Walter, was born in Brunswick County, Virginia on June 3, 1879 to Abraham and Elsie Weaver. My grandmother, Mamie, was born February 20, 1889 to Tom and Mary Dickens.

When my grandparents were married on December 26, 1906 in Greensville County, my grandmother was just 17 years old. The newlyweds rode in a beautifully decorated horse-drawn buggy to the depot where they would catch the train which was to take them to Philadelphia for their honeymoon. They were accompanied to the station by loud, upbeat music from the Masonic Temple Marching Band.

Twenty-seven-year-old Walter was a barber and independent contractor. Shortly after getting married, he purchased plot #38 on South Main Street where he erected three buildings. The one facing South Main Street was used for his family, the second was a rental unit, and the third was occupied by his mother-in-law, Mary Dickens Pebbles, who sublet to roomers and boarders, as many households did back then.

The couple had six children: Elsie, Walter, Jr., Esther Ruth, Thomas Abraham, Tessie, and Turner. Walter passed his business acumen down to his two older sons and they learned how to operate successful businesses.

After the death of my grandfather, "Mama," as I fondly called my grandmother, was faced with the responsibility of caring for her two youngest children, Tessie (my mother) and Turner. This, no doubt, was an arduous task for a widow. However, because she was a Christian and an avid Bible reader, I can imagine her walking around the house praying and singing, "The Lord will make a way somehow." Congressman Adam Clayton Powell, Jr. had not yet risen to prominence so she would not have heard him challenge those who faced hard times with his famous line: "What's in your hands?" Powell, who was also a pastor, would often urge people to look inside themselves and find ways to be creative and self-sufficient. He often referred to the biblical prophet Moses who, with God's help, used the staff in his hand to perform miracles which eventually set the Hebrew people free from Egyptian bondage.

It seems that's exactly what Mama did. She took the initiative and went uptown to the county clerk's office where "a nice lady" told her what she needed to do regarding taxes and other business matters. When her own mother, Mary Dickens Peebles died, Mama acquired Mary's roomers and boarders who lived in the third house. This was in addition to her share of rental income from a barber shop operated by her son Thomas. Affectionately, I called him "Uncle Tom." Mama and Uncle Tom were the best business partners. He had an easy-going temperament and everyone loved him. When Colored children living in the rural part of Greensville County were denied bus transportation to the high school in town, Mama provided room and board to many of them on weekdays. In 1934, several Colored parents in the county purchased school buses and charged 27 cents per week per family for transportation to the local high school.

Mama, the consummate entrepreneur, capitalized on the location of our home at 115 South Main Street, Emporia. We lived in the second house south of the U.S. Post Office.

Emporia is centrally and strategically located near most major Middle Atlantic and Eastern Seaboard states. Prior to 1959, two major highways provided access north to south by Route 301 (Main Street) and east to west by Route 58. This transportation corridor allowed Mama to have access to Colored travelers who were not allowed, by law, to stay in "white" hotels. At first, many of our guests were referred by personnel at the Belfield Hotel, a few blocks away and across the Meherrin River. Later, Mama had her own drawing card. She proudly installed an illuminated sign that read, "M.L. Weaver's Colored Tourist Home."

Many wealthy, white people traveled with their Colored maids and butlers. Unlike the Colored people, the whites did not have to use the Green Book, a travel guide designed specifically for Colored motorists. The guide was conceived by Victor H. Green, a Black New York City employee, in response to the humiliation, prejudice, and violence that Blacks faced as they traveled across the country during the Jim Crow South. Published from 1939 until

1964 when the Civil Rights Act was enacted, it listed restaurants, tourist homes, hotels, gas stations, and other accommodations in many cities in the South and West, where Colored people were welcomed. I searched the Ford Foundation Collections and Digital Collection at The Schomburg Center for Research in Black Culture on the internet, and regrettably did not find a listing for Emporia, Virginia. In more recent years, the Green Book again came to light with the publication of Calvin Alexander Ramsey's delightful children's book (2010), *Ruth and the Green Book*.

Growing up in the M.L. Weaver's Colored Tourist Home produced a lot of interesting stories. My mother, Tessie, recalled the occasion when a guest, Aunt Jemima, stayed at our house and hung her panties to dry in the bathroom. Years later, when my mother told my niece, Ayana, that Aunt Jemima had holes in her panties, possibly because she received low wages and could not afford to buy new ones, Ayana promptly cited this incident in a genealogical school report. I, like many, believed that there was only one Aunt Jemima, but that is not true. Aunt Jemima is a pseudonym for the caricature of a smiling Black-faced Colored woman wearing a red head-rag. Today, the pancake label has a more acceptable image of Aunt Jemima.

Entrepreneurism ran thick in my grandmother's blood, and her spirit of creativity was always alive and kicking. What was in Mamie Weaver's hands? Her husband was dead. Mama had a decision to make. She and Uncle Tom thought about the land grandfather owned, now their inheritance, on the north side of town. That property was on Halifax Street next to Greensville County Training School, the Colored high school. A portion of the property had been subdivided and sold to individuals who were friends of grandfather. As an independent contractor, he had built many houses in Greensville and surrounding counties. On the remaining land, Mama and Uncle Tom decided to build a dance hall, the Southern Club, because there was no facility in that area where Colored people were welcomed. Uncle Bubba (Walter, Jr.) built the hall, with a concession in the front section of the building, and Mama sold tickets at the door.

As a child I was present at most of the dances because Mama rarely found a reliable babysitter to keep me and my little sister, Elsie, who had come to live with us when she was about three or four years old. During those events, there was much excitement as both white and Colored people came out to enjoy themselves. Yet, despite the merriment, a rope was used to separate the races. The bands always brought chorus girls with them to present a floor show. Both men and women pushed to get a good view and so did I because I was curious to see what all the fuss was about.

Uncle Tom soon morphed from barber to booking agent, successfully contracting major bands such as Count Basie, Hot Lips Page, The International Sweethearts of Rhythm, Louis Jordan, and Cab Calloway to appear at the Southern Club. Back then, Colored entertainers referred to their tours through the South as "The Chitlin' Circuit."

Mama was forever seeking opportunities to support her family and to fulfill the needs of the community. It was therefore no surprise when she opened a café across the street from our home, on property owned by the Carrington family, one of the three Colored families living on Main Street. The other family was the Kemps. Prior to that, Main Street had absolutely no places where Colored people could eat. Both residents and travelers were compelled to travel across town (over the river) to the north side for a sit-down meal, or a cup of coffee at two Colored-owned and -operated restaurants. Both restaurant owners were friends of Mama. The Mid Way Café on Atlantic Avenue was a mother and son operation run by Lillian Sims and James "Jimmy" Green, and the Dew Drop Inn on Halifax Street was owned by Mary Pelham, assisted by her niece. The restaurants served delicious food and were spacious, well- appointed, and clean. Brawling was not tolerated in either place. In addition to the restaurants, Daniel and Ethel Wilkins, the parents of one of my high school classmates, owned and operated a small eatery, Wilkins' Luncheonette on Halifax Street.

As a child, I found one incident in Mama's café hilarious. There were two brothers who would get drunk every Friday after pay day. One day the younger man ordered dinner but was too intoxicated to feed himself. When he refused to leave, due to his inability to walk, Mama casually picked him up by the seat of his pants, walked to the back porch and threw him out. This courageous woman had no need for a bouncer.

CHAPTER 2

Early Childhood

MY MOTHER, TESSIE, THE YOUNGEST daughter of Walter and Mamie Weaver, married Will B. Johnson at the age of seventeen. Not long after my birth the couple separated never to see each other again. She never used her married name. She relocated to Washington, DC and he to Newport News, Virginia, leaving me to be raised in the family home in Emporia by her mother. Tessie's younger brother, Turner, gave me the nickname "Baby Bear." He died when I was too young to remember him, but the name stayed with me for a while. The boys next door took great delight in using my nickname, and when I complained, Mama asked them to stop. Next, they began to call me Mamie Ethel and finally, Ethel, when I began high school. They were the brothers of my best friend, Iris Kemp. Today, I look back and think of that teasing as brotherly love.

In the small Colored community where we lived, the Kemps, the Weavers, and the Carringtons were on South Main Street; the Greens and the Spruills lived near Shiloh Baptist Church, on the north side of Shiloh Street; and the Walkers and Robinsons lived on the south side of the road. Mr. Robinson owned a tailoring and cleaning establishment on the north side of Emporia. I played with his younger children, Jean and Earl. When they relocated, I never saw them again.

Iris and I spent our waking hours playing outside. We decorated mud pies and cakes with rose petals, tied string to the legs of June bugs pretending they were kites, we put fireflies into mason jars with holes in the lids and made lanterns, and on snowy days and nights we used corrugated boxes and sleighed merrily down the hilly lawns of the Presbyterian church and the elementary and high schools across the street, institutions of learning that we could not legally attend.

June German Celebration

Iris and I enjoyed waving to passengers on trains that traversed Greensville County on the Atlantic Coast line railroad near Shiloh Baptist Church and not far from our homes. We waved to passengers on the trains as they traveled north to south and vice versa. On Main Street (Route 301), we waved to Colored people who were heading to Rocky Mount, North Carolina to attend the annual June German, a carnival-like affair where thousands of participants danced the jitterbug all night to the music of top notch bands until they were exhausted. The people smiled and returned our greeting. We were excited because we knew that everyone in Greensville County was planning to go there also. Passing cars had license plates from New York, New Jersey, Connecticut, Delaware, Pennsylvania, and as far away as Massachusetts. When June German was on, Mama had a very hard time finding a babysitter on those nights.

CHAPTER 3

Learning from the Elders

MISS ROXIE

SOMETIMES WHEN MAMA WAS OUT of town on official duty as Daughter Rule of the Elk Lodge, Elsie and I stayed with Miss Roxie Spencer. Years before, Uncle Bubba had eloped with Miss Roxie's older daughter, Elvira. It was referred to as an elopement because Miss Roxie didn't know about it! Mama knew because she was there (with me by her side) when Rev. Pelham married them in his home. Little children have big eyes and ears...

Miss Roxie lived on the north side of town where a bumpy, dirt road off Halifax Street led up a hill to her house and farm. I was terrified each time we visited at night because the road went through the middle of Cottage Cemetery. The car got stuck frequently when it snowed. And if that wasn't scary enough, Miss Roxie and one of her friends thoroughly enjoyed telling ghost stories about headless men and horseless wagons.

After saying hello to Miss Roxie and my cousin, Junnie, I would run to the pigpen to observe the hogs and piglets as they wallowed in mud, ate slop, and drank from the trough. Although I did not witness hogs being slaughtered, I often saw the meat hanging from the ceiling while being smoked and cured in the smokehouse. I continued my exploration by plucking and eating sweet apples, pears, peaches and plums from the orchard. I was particularly fascinated by how a network of string was woven through wooden sticks and artfully placed at intervals to facilitate the upward climb of string beans as they grew. When I became an adult, I also used this technique.

Miss Green

Miss Green, one of the senior citizens in the community, made lye soap every year. This soap was used to wash dishes, clothes, and floors. Each family contributed a certain quantity of reusable frying grease which would determine how much soap they would receive. In the yard, she placed a huge, black cast iron pot over a pit of fire, added a large quantity of water into which she poured a can of Red Devil lye and the grease, and began stirring constantly. Like brew in a witch's cauldron, the mixture would spit and bubble until it thickened. When the process was over, it was spread on a hard surface to cool, and then it was cut into bars the next day.

Miss Josephine and Miss Florence

Snuff and chewing tobacco, the precursors of cigarettes, contain nicotine and some men and women used both as a way to relax or to get a mild "high." A few of the female senior citizens, including Miss Josephine and Miss Florence, used me as their errand girl. They would remove money, hidden and rolled up in the top of their thick, cotton stockings and give me instructions to buy a specific brand of snuff. I also purchased tobacco for those who smoked corn cob pipes. I was quite happy to be paid one cent for my efforts and spent it on candy immediately.

CHAPTER 4

Saving The Chickens

ONE SUMMER WHEN I WAS about five years old, it seemed the heavens opened up and poured out more water than the earth could hold. The hot August sun gave way to such an intense and incessant rain that a radio announcer reported that Virginia was experiencing the heaviest rainfall in its history, because more than six inches of rain had fallen within 12 hours. It was the Great Flood of 1940. My family sat and listened intently to the radio for details and updates. Since we lived so close to the Meherrin River, it was not unusual to see the water rise in the ditch near one of our houses when it rained for a long period of time. But this time was different. The flood water rose higher than usual, and the rain seemed as if it would never let up. Our entire household was on edge. They were jittery not only because there could be damage to our property, but also because Mama had just received a mail order of Plymouth and Leghorn baby chicks. The chickens were placed in a pen that was enclosed with wire, but due to the severity of the flood, the chicks had to be transferred to the back porch. At that point, Mama and Uncle Tom sent me to stay with friends while they remained at home to protect the property.

The river rose so high that people traveling on Route 301 had to make a detour. Later when the rains subsided, residents on both sides of the river ventured out to see how much damage was done. Some used the opportunity to go out in boats, while others took to swimming. One boat overturned, but fortunately Uncle Tom managed to rescue the occupants. Thanks be to God, our house suffered no significant damage.

CHAPTER 5

Religion and Politics

REVIVALS

THE PEOPLE OF GREENSVILLE COUNTY anticipated the arrival of three major events every year—revivals, the Silas Green Show, and the Ringling Bros. and Barnum and Bailey Circus. For me, revivals were the most exciting. In most instances, revivals took place in Baptist and Holiness churches and continued for a week. Church officials coordinated dates with each other to avoid conflict in scheduling and thus allow members to attend each other's revival. Most of the preachers were from Virginia and North Carolina, which is only eighteen miles from Virginia's border.

Revivals were so popular that people called backsliders, those who stayed away from the church and strayed from their faith, were drawn back to church – at least for a week. As a child, I never understood why they were called backsliders because they usually sat up front and shouted louder than the regular congregants. Although several charismatic preachers were invited, I remember one in particular who mesmerized the crowd. He titled his sermons after popular secular songs such as, "I Heard You Crying in the Chapel," and "When the Swallows Come Back to Capistrano." He and other preachers energized the crowd by incorporating what is called "whooping" in their sermons. Used primarily in the Black church, especially near the end of the sermon, although it can occur at any point, whooping is a type of vocal musical inflection, like a chant or holler mixed with a singsong sound that creates a dramatic guttural effect. This preacher was so captivating that I myself often felt like shouting.

Black Barbers

Like the preachers, barbers played an important role in the African-American community. My grandfather's generation of Black barbers was not the first to profit from their trade. Before the Civil War, Black barbers made most of their money shaving and cutting the hair of white clients. It was a skill these men acquired and it earned them an honest living. Many barbers used their earnings to purchase real estate to help them move up the social ladder. As a popular saying in the Black community goes, "If you don't know where you came from, you won't know where you're going." The barbershop was a place where men, young and old, gathered to talk about their struggles. It was a place where they congregated to discuss what it was like to be a man, in an arena where it was safe to pass down words of wisdom to the young men who would eventually take their place. It was a place to share their history.

Today, equal rights and justice advocates encourage African Americans to know their history because it is not Black history, but American history. Knowing the history of how Black barbers evolved over the years makes me proud to be the granddaughter and niece of barbers. I was born and raised in a building that was both a home and a barbershop, and it was built by my grandfather's own two hands. The Bible is right when it declares that a good man leaves an inheritance for his children's children.

Sometimes Mama would sit and read *The Journal and Guide, Richmond News Leader, Richmond Dispatch, The Crisis* magazine (a publication of the NAACP) or the Bible. I would often sit beside her, but if business was slow at the barbershop I would go there to amuse myself. I enjoyed spinning around in the barber's chair, whizzing at a dizzying speed like a human top. I also loved listening to music from the piccolo (jukebox), and watching Edward Barner shine shoes. When he didn't have a customer, I'd pretend I was having my shoes shined. When customers came for haircuts, I returned to take my place near the "reading lady."

During baseball season everyone in the barbershop discussed the games as they listened to the radio. At other times, they discussed politics. The discussions centered mostly around school desegregation and voting rights. All I could hear about was poll taxes. School teachers and other Colored people were asked to count beans in a bottle and recite the Constitution. Uncle Tom and some other civic-minded men drove throughout Greensville County urging people to pay the poll tax so that they could vote. Voting restrictions and the lack of transportation to high school for children in the rural community were critical factors that propelled citizens to join the National Association for the Advancement of Colored People (NAACP). Dr. F.A. Sealy, a dentist from North Carolina, came to Emporia and organized farmers, ministers, teachers, beauticians, morticians, lawyers, doctors, and local business owners to form a chapter of this civil rights organization. On June 10, 1940, Emporia-Greensville became a branch of the NAACP.

I was told that the NAACP charter documentation materialized when Mr. Steve J. Ackerman, a journalist, came upon it in the

Library of Congress while doing research on attorney S.W. Tucker. Mrs. Rose Person Allen's name was among the papers and he contacted her. Mrs. Allen, who died in 2010, was a stalwart activist and a dedicated educator. My uncles, Thomas A. Weaver and Walter H. Weaver II, were two of the sixty-five members that signed the charter. [See list of members (Appendix I).]

CHAPTER 6

A Time to Celebrate
and to Serve

APRIL 2, 1941 WAS A typical day in Virginia with sunshine and intermittent showers. It was my sixth birthday and Mama and some of the ladies in the neighborhood were busy making preparations for my birthday party. I was wearing a beautiful dress that Miss Estelle Wiggins had made for me. Miss Rosa, a lady who came twice a week to help Mama with the cleaning, was there also.

Uncle Tom, who now owned a taxicab business, and several of his drivers were responsible for providing door-to-door service for guests attending my birthday party. It was a fabulous affair, and everyone had a great time. One incident, however, marred the happy occasion. Harry Parker kissed me on the cheek and, embarrassed, I hid under the dining room table. One of my guests, Virginia Lee Ellis, ran to tell the adults what had happened.

Six months after my birthday, Uncle Tom was drafted into the Army. One by one, all of the barbers in the shop were drafted and Mama and I were alone, except for a boarder and a roomer who were too old to serve. During World War II, the military converted a large building on South Main Street into a factory. It had been a

17

used car dealership, but was now being used to supply the military with tents. While it provided local women, white and Black, with employment, it fed my childlike curiosity with several new and exciting experiences. Since everyone knew me, I was allowed to walk around and observe various stages of tent-making. Sometimes I was even allowed to place brass rings on heavy tent fabric using an instrument to punch holes in the fabric. Later, the soldiers would drive stakes through these holes when they were setting up the tents. At this time Emporia and Greensville County women were part of the "Rosie the Riveter" era, a period during which women did what was traditionally a man's job while the men were serving in the military.

CHAPTER 7

Camp Pickett

IN LATE 1941, AS WAR drew closer to America's shores, a team of Army surveyors visited the site of a former civilian conservation corps camp near the small rural town of Blackstone, Virginia. There they found enough land, water, and other resources needed to establish a post large enough to simultaneously train more than one infantry division. The site also offered easy railroad access to both mountain and coastal training sites.

By December 1941, some 45,867 acres of land in Nottoway, Dinwiddie, Lunenburg, and Brunswick counties were acquired by imminent domain and cleared to be prepared for construction of the first buildings of Fort Pickett, locally known as Camp Pickett. These lands were owned by predominantly African-American communities. According to relatives living in Dinwiddie, Virginia, my paternal great-great grandfather, Robert Michael and my great-great uncle, William Henry Michael, and their extended families were buried there in cemeteries at Birch Hill Baptist Church and Spring Hill Baptist Church, respectively. When the land was cleared, approximately 1,400 bodies were exhumed and re-interred in Gills Bridge Road Cemetery.

CHAPTER 8

A Long Walk for Education

THE ROSENWALD SCHOOLS

R.R. MOTON ELEMENTARY SCHOOL AND Greensville County Training School were known as Rosenwald schools because they were partially financed by Julius Rosenwald, a millionaire who was president of Sears and Roebuck stores. It is believed that Booker T. Washington's Tuskegee Institute was the first recipient of Rosenwald's philanthropy to benefit African-American education in the South in 1912.

By 1928, one in every five rural schools for Black students in the South was a Rosenwald school. At the program's end in 1932, there were 4,977 new schools, 217 teachers' residences and 163 shop buildings, constructed at a total cost of $28,408,520 to serve 663,615 students in 883 counties of 15 states.

In 1929, a six-teacher planned school was constructed in Emporia. The community contributed $1,000, the Rosenwald Fund $1,700, and the public contributed $12,419.[1]

R.R. MOTON ELEMENTARY SCHOOL

Although my family lived directly across the street from Emporia Elementary and Emporia High Schools, it was against the law for me to attend those schools. Instead, I walked several miles to attend R.R. Moton Elementary School uptown. Six years later, I again walked miles to attend Greensville County Training School, the high school for Colored children on the north side of town.

There were rules governing which side of the street children were allowed to use when walking to and from school. In the morning, Colored children walked on the west side of Main Street and white children walked on the east side, to avoid fights. In the afternoon, whites walked on the west side and Coloreds on the east side. One morning, I was late and walking alone to school on the correct side of the street when I was approached by a tall, skinny white boy who, without provocation, slapped me. I turned around, ran back home and promptly told Mama about the incident. I recognized him because he lived on Clay Street, across the street from friends of ours. Mama knew the boy's mother because she had made several garments for me. Calmly, she went to the boy's house and told his mother what had happened. The woman promptly apologized for her son's behavior.

GREENSVILLE COUNTY TRAINING SCHOOL

I enjoyed elementary school very much and I loved high school as well. There, I joined the Glee Club and the basketball team. Everyone expected me to join the Glee Club because I sang in the junior choir at Royal Baptist Church, and was one of the soloists. I inherited my ability to sing from Mama. She sang in the senior choir. Uncle Tom was a tenor soloist at Shiloh Baptist Church. Sometimes Mama sang duets with Mrs. Leslie Tucker who sang alto. I loved to hear them sing together, and so did the congregation. Mama told me that Mrs. Tucker was a cousin of the renowned singer Pearl Bailey. I knew from entertainment magazines that Pearl Bailey was from Newport News, Virginia, and so was the Tucker Family. Years later, I confirmed this information with one of Mrs. Tucker's granddaughters.

In the 1950s, just as it is today, basketball was the primary source of recreation in the South. My girlfriends and I joined the basketball team in high school. Our team traveled by school bus at night to other schools in our district and to other towns in Virginia and North Carolina.

During a game in Ahoskie, North Carolina I sustained an injury that sidelined me for weeks. A girl on the opposing team tripped me intentionally, causing me to fracture my left mandible. With my jawbone injured, I was in excruciating pain. When I returned home that night, I was rushed to the hospital in nearby Weldon, North Carolina because there were no hospitals in Emporia. Doctors at the hospital wrapped bandages around my head and chin leaving a small opening around my mouth to allow for sipping liquids.

During my recuperation, I learned a new word when Mama instructed my sister to go to the drug store and purchase a "quill," a glass straw, that would be used to feed me pureed or soft foods. Dr. Adams made daily home visits to administer penicillin injections, and my friends visited me in my room. Our principal, Mr. Frank Smith, visited also.

Boys and girls on the basketball team, especially those in my class, took their academic responsibilities seriously. Mr. Smith did not postpone exams that were scheduled the morning following out-of-town games, and we had to find the time and place where we could study during games. The girls' team studied during the boys' game and vice versa.

At one point in Greensville County, high school education only went through the tenth grade. According to Uncle Tom's classmate Mrs. Effie Foster Revis, when another year of instruction was added, their class was the first class to graduate from the eleventh grade. My own class was on track to graduate in 1952 from the eleventh grade, but that was not to be. The superintendent of schools for Greensville County mandated that Greensville County Training School would graduate the first five-year class in 1953, thereby allowing us to be the first class to graduate in the twelfth grade. The Class of 1953 continued its ground-breaking activities by spearheading Greensville County Training School's first high school band, and its first football and cheerleading teams. We chose royal blue and orange as the school's colors, and named our athletic teams, the Panthers.

I was president of my class for four years, losing out in the fifth year. I was also voted prom queen and attended the 1952 ROTC Ball at Virginia State College with Chauncey Phillips, a friend of my ex-boyfriend. As a freshman, I was invited to attend the inaugural parade of President Harry S. Truman with the senior class. Four years later, I attended the inaugural parade of President Eisenhower with my own senior classmates.

Ten years later, I would have another presidential encounter. After graduating from Harlem Hospital School of Nursing, my pastor, Rev. Hylton James, Sr. of Berean Missionary Baptist Church asked me and Melvin Thompson, a funeral director and member of the church, to organize a blood bank for the members. We contacted the American Red Cross and together we sponsored a successful blood drive. Later, we were invited to a reception where President Eisenhower was the guest speaker.

CHAPTER 9

Dating and "Good Livers"

IN HIGH SCHOOL, I WAS attracted to a good-looking boy who was four years my senior and became anxious when he asked me if he could visit me at home. A girl in my class had informed me that he was seeing another girl in the rural section of the county where he lived. When I asked Mama for permission for him to visit me, before she gave an answer she asked me, "Who is his family? Are they good livers?" The next time I saw him, I asked him about his family. He told me his grandfather's name and that he owned a large farm with hired hands; his mother and my Aunt Elsie attended school together; and his older sister was attending Virginia State College. Mama and Uncle Tom knew the family and gave their approval.

Since then, I've never heard anyone use the phrase "good livers." Mama was, of course, referring to the background of the family of my would-be suitor. Is his family God-fearing? Are they industrious? Are they of good character and reputation? Although these questions may seem intrusive, it is important for parents to know the background of people with whom their children are closely associated.

CHAPTER 10

Fighting the War in Korea and Segregration at Home

ONE SUNDAY MORNING, FOUR SOLDIERS who were stationed in Blackstone, Virginia at Camp Pickett, attended services at Royal Baptist Church while in town for a baseball game. Rev. Shands welcomed the visitors and introduced them to the congregation. After church, the soldiers joined a few choir members, including me, at Dr. Joyner's Colored Pharmacy and Soda Fountain.

Although I didn't care much for baseball, I decided to go with Uncle Tom to the game that Sunday. He was one of the managers of Emporia's team. By the time the game ended, I had exchanged telephone numbers with Stephen, a soldier, who was originally from Detroit. From that day, he traveled to visit me every Sunday until he was deployed overseas. During this time, the government and the Red Cross were urging the public to support the troops with letters and care packages. I was inspired by a cookie recipe on a Baby Ruth candy bar and asked Mama for permission to make and send cookies to Stephen. By doing this, I felt as if I had made some small contribution to uplift the morale of Stephen and his barrack mates.

In the summer of 1952, I visited my mother in Washington D.C. and got in touch with a colleague from school who was vacationing there. My friend arranged for me to join her and a couple of boys from home, whom I did not know, for a night out. They were now soldiers stationed at Fort Meade in Alexandria, Virginia.

We laughed, talked, and danced at the club on the Army base. I love to dance and seldom missed an opportunity to do so. Therefore, I didn't hesitate to dance when young men dressed in Air Force uniform asked me to dance once or twice. The situation became contentious and the conversation between the young men moved from the dance floor and continued outside. In retrospect, maybe I should have asked, "Are your families 'good livers'?" Jealousy was not the only cause of friction.

That same year the United States was engaged in the Korean War. The U.S. Armed Services was segregated, and at times there was animosity between branches of the military because one had privileges that the other did not have. For example, the Air Force became integrated before the Army. As a matter of fact, the Army was more recalcitrant than any of the other branches of the Armed Services in terms of segregation.

Four years prior to my Fort Meade experience, on July 26, 1948, President Harry Truman signed Executive Order 9981, establishing the President's Committee on Equality of Treatment and Opportunity in the Armed Services. The final step did not occur until the publication of Department of Defense directive 5120.36 on July 26, 1963 some 15 years after President Truman signed his original order. Credit must, however, be given to the many unsung heroes who fought persistently after World War II to end segregation in the Armed Services. Their speeches and their writings did not go unheeded. Notably among them were A. Phillip Randolph and Mary McCleod Bethune.

CHAPTER 11

Judged by the Color
of Their Skin

⁓

THE ISSUES SURROUNDING VOTER REGISTRATION and school de-segregation were not the only injustices towards people of color during the 1950s and 1960s. Thalhimers and Miller and Rhoades department stores refused to issue credit cards to financially-worthy Black applicants. These were the two most prominent department stores in Richmond, the capital of Virginia. Mama and Aunt Terris, Uncle Tom's wife, were furious about this matter, almost as much as they were about poll taxes.

Many families in Emporia subscribed to The Richmond News Leader and The Richmond Dispatch and saw advertisements of beautiful dresses, shoes, and other items they desired. Colored people were allowed to shop in these stores but were barred from using the water fountains, bathrooms, or dressing rooms. I vividly recall when Aunt Terris took my friend Iris and me to Thalhimer's department store to buy our first pair of high heel shoes. We sat down in the shoe department and tried on several pair of shoes until I settled for a green pair and Iris for a blue one. Yet, I also painfully remember times when Mama, Aunt Terris, and I had to leave the store, and drive to the Colored section of the city on Market Street, in order to eat and use the bathroom. When the owners of these department stores were chided about their policy of segregation, they nonchalantly replied that they had to adhere to the laws of the state.

A few years later, however, things began to change. In 1960, thirty-four students from the then all-Colored Virginia Union University, successfully boycotted Thalhimer's, Miller and Rhoades, and several other businesses. The students, later known as the Richmond 34, marched and picketed Thalhimer's and staged a sit-in at the store's lunch counter. All were arrested but were bailed out by the Black community. The community kept the pressure up by continuing to picket and boycott until the stores finally adopted desegregation policies.

CHAPTER 12

Welcome to Harlem Hospital School of Nursing (1953-1956)

SEPTEMBER 9, 1953 WAS A momentous occasion for my grandmother, Mamie Louise Weaver, for she had successfully nurtured and guided me to this point in time where I would become a professional nurse. She escorted me through the door of Harlem Hospital School of Nursing's residence at 27 West 136th Street, located between Lenox and Fifth Avenues in Harlem, New York. We took the elevator to the 9th floor where my classmates and I, each had separate rooms. Satisfied, Mama went to Brooklyn to spend time with her daughters, Esther Banks and Elsie Carter.

I joined my classmates in the student's Health Service Department to be examined and to receive the necessary immunizations. There were sixty-four students in my class when we started, but only forty-one graduated three years later. The teaching staff at Harlem Hospital School of Nursing was very demanding, but even at 18 years old, I was a serious student. "Dear God, please don't let me disappoint Mama," was my fervent prayer each night. I knew that she and my family had aspirations of me being "The Great Black Hope" of our family because I was an honor student in high school. I was to be a role model for my cousins, Lynn and Tommy, who like me, were born in the family home in Emporia. I was to be the first in the family to graduate from an institution of higher education. Years before, my Aunt Elsie was matriculated at Virginia State College, but quit more than once, without parental consent. My grandfather located her in New York, brought her back and she left again. Her explanation was that she didn't have beautiful clothes like the daughters of doctors and lawyers. She remained a *fashionista* for the rest of her life.

A BRIEF HISTORY OF HARLEM HOSPITAL SCHOOL OF NURSING

The school historian, Mrs. Mildred Christina Norman, who was one of my former medical instructors, revealed an integral part of the school's history of which I was unaware. It is said that Mr. Vassall, a Colored man, had four daughters, one of whom wanted to be a registered nurse. Nearby Bellevue Hospital, established in May 1837, did not accept Colored girls. Mr. Vassall spent years appealing to the authorities to open a school for Colored girls. Finally, on January 1, 1923, the Harlem Hospital School of Nursing was opened and two and a half years later, his daughter, Lurline, was among the first graduating class. Today, fewer than 100 hospital-based programs, like Harlem Hospital's School of Nursing, are available for students due to the availability and popularity of Associate Degree and Bachelor of Science Degree programs. (See Appendix 2).

Another of Mr. Vassall's daughters who became a medical doctor, lived next door to my Aunt Esther on Putnam Avenue in Brooklyn. She was our family doctor. I didn't know about her sister, Lurline, at that time, but many years later, I met her at the school's class reunions. What a small world!

During my tenure at nursing school, I attended Berean Baptist Church in Brooklyn on Sundays. At other times, when I was hard pressed for time and had exams, I attended nearby Abyssinian Baptist Church where Rev. Adam Clayton Powell, Jr. was pastor. When he entered the pulpit, the congregants greeted him with heartfelt enthusiasm because he was not there every Sunday since he was also a congressman who served in the House of Representatives in Washington, DC. Rev. Powell was a gifted orator who kept his audience abreast of community and national affairs. He was well-known for empowering people by encouraging them to utilize their talent, and to take advantage of their right to voice their concerns as citizens, and to make full use of their right to vote. Over the years, I have learned that it is incumbent upon us to march, demonstrate, and advocate if we want to have access and share in the American Dream.

HARLEM'S SOAPBOX ORATORS

Students at Harlem Hospital School of Nursing could spend all three years of nursing training without ever leaving the building. The nurses' residence and the hospital were connected by a tunnel in the basement. On a few occasions when I decided to venture out to Lenox Avenue, I was surprised to see a man on the corner of Lenox Avenue and 135th Street standing on a platform speaking to a crowd of people who listened attentively. At first I thought the man was a preacher, but soon realized he was talking politics.

Some years later, I realized that I had witnessed a very important part of history in the struggle for equal justice in the United

States. A. Phillip Randolph is known to have spoken at this corner during the time I was in nursing school. He later founded the Brotherhood of Sleeping Car Porters. I would like to think that he was one of the men I witnessed on the soapbox. Years earlier, Marcus Mosiah Garvey, political activist and civil rights leader, spoke on the very same corner.

NIGHT LIFE

New York is known as the city that never sleeps. The nursing school was only two or three blocks from the legendary Savoy Ballroom and we were granted free admission before 10 pm. I always thought this was a way to entice young men who could rely on having dance partners. I loved to dance and attended frequently. Quite often couples on the dance floor were doing the Jitterbug and the Lindy Hop, while others were practicing for an annual competition.

Periodically, famous entertainers appeared at The Savoy. I was there one night when Nat "King" Cole was expected to appear. The joint was jumping. People on the dance floor stretched their necks looking toward the entrance. Those who were sitting at tables were leaning over, looking towards the door. I was standing near the door when Mr. Cole, surrounded by his entourage swept by me. I got instant goose bumps. There I was in the same room as the incomparable singer Nat "King" Cole. It was truly an unforgettable experience.

My classmate, Rachael Goodin, a Harlemite who enjoyed dancing as much as I did, invited me to go with her to watch a dance competition downtown. All of the couples were white; the women wore beautiful gowns and costumes and the men wore tuxedos. They gracefully danced the waltz, gliding across the ballroom floor in what seemed like effortless movements, or led their partners through the precise steps of the foxtrot. Suddenly, near the end of the program, a Colored couple burst onto the stage—the woman wore a skirt and blouse, and the man wore a shirt with rolled-up sleeves and pants, both wore saddle laced-up shoes with white socks. They danced the Lindy Hop, having practiced at the Savoy Ballroom. I was mortified. This couple appeared to be allowed in the competition solely as entertainment for the others. Why were there no Colored people in other dance categories? Humiliated, I understood why Rachael and I were the only people of color in the auditorium.

A few weeks later, Rachael took me to a ballroom to hear Tito Puente, a famous Hispanic musician. As a girl from a small town in the South, I had neither seen nor met any Hispanic people before and was not familiar with their music. All that changed the night I walked into the Palladium. The music was fast and rhythmic and I loved it. A young man pulled Rachael onto the dance floor, while I was left explaining to another young man, "I don't know how to do the Rumba or the Calypso." Despite my protests, each young man said, "Don't worry, I'll teach you." When I left the ballroom that night I had mastered both dances. It just goes to show that dance is a universal language.

CASE STUDY: DISCOVERY OF STREPTOMYCIN

During my internship on the male medical ward at Harlem Hospital, I was assigned to a Korean War veteran who had been diagnosed with tuberculosis. He did not know whether or not his wife and children were dead or alive. Because Harlem Hospital was located in a predominantly Black community, it was quite unusual to see a Korean there. At first I wondered why my patient was not admitted to the designated tuberculosis hospital, Sea View, located on Staten Island. It was there that my schoolmates and I lived in residence for several months with nursing students from other schools to learn the treatment and care of patients with tuberculosis.

I was responsible for the complete care of the patient. He was pleasant, spoke English, and related well with the staff and other patients. He did not exhibit any signs of depression or speak of his family further. He responded well to treatment and when able to walk, he met me at the elevator each morning. I'm sure he was aware that my classmates found his behavior hilarious.

Dr. Selman Waksman discovered Streptomycin, the cure for tuberculosis in 1943, and won the Nobel Prize in 1952. Later, when the tubercular bacteria became resistant to Streptomycin, other drugs were introduced so that patients no longer had to spend months, even years in sanatoriums, such as Sea View Hospital.

LIFE AFTER NURSING SCHOOL

After graduation, I remained at Harlem Hospital for a year as a surgical nurse in Pediatrics, commuting from Brooklyn where I lived with my aunt Esther. I spent the next two years as a Head Nurse of Neurosurgery in "F" building at Kings County Hospital. Later, I became affiliated with the New York City Department of Health and was assigned to a Brooklyn District Office as a Public Health nurse. At that time, Public Health nurses were largely responsible for school health, clinic assignments which included sexually transmitted diseases (STDs) and tuberculosis, child health stations, and home visits.

These nurses were expected to go into "the field" when schools closed at three o'clock in the afternoon. One day, in 1972, when I visited a home because the parents had failed to bring their child for an appointment at the tuberculosis clinic, the child's mother stated that her son was still at Willowbrook Hospital (Willowbrook State School for Children with Intellectual Disabilities), and that he contracted tuberculosis there. She showed me a photograph of her son, who seemed to be about 10 years old, and who was more pretty than handsome. In distress, the mother told me, "One day when I visited my son on the open ward, I found a boy in bed with him, fondling him." Needless to say, I was shocked by this account and submitted a written report to my supervisor the following morning. I never received feedback from my supervisor. However, a few months later, reporter Geraldo Rivera broke the story about gross abuse, both physical and sexual, which had taken place at Willowbrook.

Actually, this was not news to families of the intellectually disabled patients there. They, and some of the facility's employees, had complained about the overcrowding and filthy conditions to which patients were subjected. As a nurse who has worked in various hospitals, I am well aware that New York City Department of Health and Hospitals conducts annual inspections. However, what happened at Willowbrook Hospital at that time was reprehensible.

CHAPTER 13

A Whirlwind Tour of
Western Europe

Determined to further my education by working days and attending New York University at night, I lost all sense of time. Before I knew it, I never had a vacation other than visiting Mama in Virginia during my early working years. My first trip abroad was to Jamaica, West Indies. There I visited Montego Bay and Kingston, the capital city. I remember the exhilaration of dancing in sand on the beach at night, under moon and stars that appeared so close I could almost touch them. Little did I know that I would travel extensively in the future.

My next trip, which took me to Europe, came unexpectedly during the early days of the 1960s civil rights upheaval. A chartered flight was sponsored by a civil rights organization from Manhattan. Joan Hicks, the cousin of my best friend, accompanied me. Joan Hughes, another passenger on the trip, lived only a few blocks from me in Brooklyn. We became lifelong friends. Upon arriving at Dulles Airport in Paris, France we were surprised to learn that half of the group would not be taking the guided tour. Mr. Smith, an elderly gentleman, met us at the airport. He was to be our guide for the entire trip.

The itinerary included many museums. Everyone was thrilled to go to the Eiffel Tower. I did not share their excitement because the structure didn't seem too stable, and neither did the Leaning Tower of Pisa in Italy! After dinner we were ready to party, but Mr. Smith tried to convince us to retire early and be ready for the next day. With help from the concierge, we were able to bypass that advice and explore safe, recreational activities later that evening— one of which was dancing. When an American girl agrees to dance with a partner, it is usually for only one dance; in France, the partner expects to keep the girl on the dance floor for a "complete set" of dances. At least that's what my partner told me. And, he wasn't even a good dancer!

When we got to Italy, the smell coming from the body of water at the Italian seaport was noxious. At that time, if I had had an alternative, I would not have boarded the waiting gondola. The gondola was decorated with flowers and the gondolier sang as he rowed through the sewage- contaminated waters. While in Venice, either the smell dissipated, or I became acclimated to it.

According to Mr. Smith, our very proficient guide, Venice was an archipelago of 117 islands formed by 177 canals in a shallow lagoon connected by bridges. In its earlier years, travel was mostly by water. The foundation of the city is made from wooden piles upon which stone and brick buildings were built.

Vatican City

When I read Irving Stone's biographical novel on Michelangelo, *The Agony and The Ecstasy*, in 1961, I had no idea I would actually set foot in Vatican City the following year. Vatican City is a sovereign city-state of The Holy See, also known as The Holy City. It is a walled enclave that houses a multitude of cathedrals and muse-ums. We walked through the sprawling piazza of St. Peter's Square within the enclave to reach St. Peter's Basilica and the Vatican, where the sitting Pope resides. The piazza was teeming with tour-ists from around the world. Among them were hundreds of nuns. I was fascinated by the extreme differences in their attire, especially the headgear known as a wimple. A cornette is a type of wimple consisting of a large piece of white cloth that is folded upwards in such a fashion as to create the resemblance of horns, or a scroll. Some were fashioned with downward folds extending to the shoul-ders or longer resembling the headgear worn in the movie, "The Flying Nun."

Vatican City's tour guide ushered our group to the end of the Vatican Museum, just north of St. Peter's Basilica where the Sistine Chapel is located. It is named for Pope Sistus who commissioned its construction in the 15th century. It is, by far, the most popular tourist attraction there. In the early 16th century, Pope Julius II commissioned Michelangelo Buonarroti, an Italian Renaissance sculptor, painter, architect and poet, who was considered the great-est artist of his day, to decorate the ceiling of the Sistine Chapel. Words cannot express how thrilled I was to be gazing up at the fres-cos depicting prophets, sibyls, and scenes from the book of Genesis on the ceiling and on the back wall of the Sistine Chapel. Having read *The Agony and The Ecstasy*, I felt as if I knew Michelangelo and that I had observed him as he worked in the Chapel.

MONACO, HOME OF MONTE CARLO

Germany and Belgium were included in our itinerary, also, Luxemburg, a French principality. We were, however, more interested in rubbing shoulders with the rich and famous in Monaco, another French principality. Monaco is bordered by France on three sides, and the Mediterranean Sea on the other. Known as the French Riviera, a resort area, it has been said that in terms of beauty, Monaco is second only to Vatican City. Like many beach resorts, Monaco has beautiful, white sandy beaches and azure beach fronts. The waters at Monaco appeared to be a launching pad for large yachts and sailboats of the rich and famous which could be seen darting about while we dined at the sprawling Monte Carlo restaurant. Next door was the legendary Monte Carlo Casino, which has been depicted in many movies.

CHAPTER 14

The Struggle for Civil Rights

HAVING RECENTLY RETURNED FROM EUROPE, I found myself in the throes of the ever-evolving civil rights struggle. I went to Concord Baptist Church in Brooklyn to hear Rev. Dr. Martin Luther King, Jr. speak at a rally. The pastor of that church, Rev. Dr. Gardner C. Taylor, was himself, a legendary orator. Throngs of activists and followers filled the sanctuary and beyond. Like others in attendance, I was mesmerized by Dr. King's presence and the intonation and cadence of his voice. Everyone left fired-up and ready to go.

On June 12, 1963, a few hours after President John F. Kennedy made one of his strongest civil rights speeches, a civil rights leader named Medgar Evers was assassinated in Mississippi by a member of the White Citizen's Council. Dr. King delivered his "I Have a Dream" speech during the August 28, 1963 March on Washington for civil rights and equal justice. The following month, on September 15, 1963, members of the Klu Klux Klan (KKK) bombed the 16th Street Baptist Church in Birmingham, Alabama killing four young girls: Addie Mae Collins, 14; Denise McNair, 11; Cynthia Wesley, 14; and Carol Robinson, 14. Two months later, violence continued to spill into murder, and President John F. Kennedy was assassinated in Texas on November 22, 1963. And, a little more than six months later, on June 21, 1964, three young civil rights volunteers were murdered by the Klan while participating in the Mississippi Freedom Summer Project. They were James Chaney, an African American, and Andrew Goodman and Michael Schwerner, both of whom were Jewish.

When President Lyndon B. Johnson signed the Civil Rights Act of 1964 outlawing discrimination in voting, public accommodations, and requiring fair employment practices, two of my friends who were extremely qualified, were promoted in their respective professions. One, a chemist, was promoted to director of the laboratory where he was employed. The other was made director of a newly-created department by a major motion picture corporation, in an attempt to reach out to the African-American community. Unfortunately, these positions were both short-lived.

CHAPTER 15

A Dream Deferred

WHILE CIVIL RIGHTS LEADERS AND activists continued to effect change, I focused on improving my vocal abilities. My vocal coaches were Professor Alexander Gatewood, choir director, and Professor Aaron Clarke, Sr., both of Berean Baptist Missionary Church in Brooklyn, where I was a member, and Mr. Chauncey Scott Northern, a graduate of Hampton Institute (now Hampton University). Mr. Northern had composed the original musical arrangement for the song, "Through Centuries Ringing," which became the University's anthem. An accomplished opera singer, Mr. Northern lived and performed abroad for many years. Upon his return to the United States, he founded the Northern Vocal Art School at Carnegie Hall where I was one of his students.

One day, approximately six students, including me, were vocalizing together when a young woman we had never seen before, entered the room. Mr. Northern introduced her to the group as Maya Angelou (Marguerite Annie Johnson). We were told that she was an actress, singer, and dancer having appeared in a play with James Earl Jones, Cicely Tyson and others. She had also toured Europe with a production of the opera "Porgy and Bess." Maya joined us in a series of vocal exercises. Much to our surprise, Maya was also an author. Each of us purchased her first edition book, *I Know Why the Caged Bird Sings*, and she autographed each one. I kept the book for many years, not knowing she would become famous. Unfortunately, I have misplaced the book, yet I refuse to believe that it is lost.

My other vocal coaches included Ms. Collins of Virginia State College and Mrs. Von Woert at The Brooklyn Conservatory of Music. Once a week I traveled by Greyhound bus to Petersburg, Virginia to study with Ms. Collins. She also taught Camilla Williams, a well-known operatic soprano, who is believed to be the first Black woman to play a leading role in a major American opera company. I made my debut recital on April 18, 1964 at The Brooklyn Academy of Music, accompanied on piano by Jonathan Brice of Manhattan. Mr. Brice's sister, Carol, was also an accomplished opera singer. The recital was sponsored by Lambda Kappa Mu Sorority, Gamma Chapter, of which I am a member.

During that time, I deferred my dream of singing and instead focused my attention on graduating from New York University with a Bachelor of Science in Nursing. Later, I would graduate from Long Island University with a Master's Degree in Community Health.

HONEYMOON: MAMA, HUGHEY, AND ME

When Mama came to New York to attend my wedding, my husband Hughey and I took her to the World's Fair of 1964-1965 in Queens, New York, the theme of which was "Peace Through Understanding." Mama had previously attended the 1939-1940 World's Fair when it was in New York. Back then, the theme was "Build the World of Tomorrow." But themes do not always reflect world conditions. The United States was in the latter phase of the Great Depression and on the verge of World War II in 1939-1940, and we were in the throes of the Civil Rights Movement in 1964-65.

A few days later, Mama, Hughey, and I journeyed to Camden, South Carolina to meet my in-laws.

CHAPTER 16

White Flight and Block-Busting

WHO KNEW THAT THE COMBINATION of home ownership and motherhood would prove problematic? It was difficult to find a neighborhood with good schools when we moved from St. Albans to Laurelton, in Queens, New York. Every day I saw moving vans, sometimes two a day, relocating white families because upper middle class African Americans were moving into the neighborhood. I remember one day bursting into tears as I watched caravans leaving 229th Street in search of all-white neighborhoods. That was my first real estate lesson.

"White flight" is a term used to describe the above phenomenon created by many real estate brokers in an attempt to scare white homeowners into giving them business. The brokers are able to make two transactions by selling one person's house and receiving a commission, then finding that same client another house and making a second commission. That is called "block busting" which is now illegal, but was tolerated then.

It is uncanny how one decision can trigger a reaction that alters the course of events in our lives. That's exactly what happened when a friend who sold her home in Laurelton and moved to California, had to return to New York if she wanted to keep the student loan for her son who was in medical school. She wrote to me requesting that I send her the listing "Houses for Sale by HUD and The VA-Bids," that was published in various newspapers. I complied and in the process of looking at properties, my husband and I decided to make an investment in one of the houses.

Applicants who wanted to purchase HUD and VA properties were required to retain a real estate broker who would submit the bid. We applied, had our bid submitted, and we won. I caught the real estate bug and was now definitely interested in getting my real estate license. New Year's Eve of the following year found me studying for the real estate exam after church. A few years after gaining experience with other real estate brokers, one of them introduced me to someone who owned a commercial property that he needed to "unload" quickly. My husband and I used the profit we made from the HUD property to purchase that commercial property, which then became our real estate office.

CHAPTER 17

Young, Gifted, and Black

Not long after my experience with "white flight" and "block busting," I turned my attention towards the education of my daughter, April. I received a letter from P.S. 56Q informing me that April, along with some of her classmates in kindergarten would be promoted to the second grade. I almost fainted and I couldn't wait to tell her father the good news when he came home. Later that semester, we received even more good news. April and the same classmates had been accepted in the Queens Association for the Education of the Exceptionally Gifted Child, Inc. (QAEEGC) in Community School District 29 housed at P.S. 95Q in Queens Village. It was a surprise since we had not applied to this program. Parents of students in Laurelton, Rosedale, and Cambria Heights were required to provide their own transportation because of the distance and the tender age of the students.

The Association was founded in 1969 by Mrs. Margery B. McCreary, a mother of two, Louis Jr. and Laurence, who lived in Hollis. In September 1970, along with NY State Education Department and York College of the City University of New York, the first class of the gifted was organized on a fifth grade level. Thirty students were drawn from approximately 11 elementary schools in Community District 29. Mrs. McCreary believed that the Intellectually Gifted Child (IGC) program that currently existed in Southeast Queens was not effective in minority communities. At the March 3, 1973 conference on QAEEGC, Mrs. McCreary said, "We felt (referring to the board) that Queens was a large enough borough and needed a program comparable to Hunter College's Elementary School in Manhattan."[2]

"A unique dimension of this project was the design for providing a competent staff to carry out the educational goals and objectives of the curriculum design. Eight professors from York College were assigned to teach their particular discipline. These professors traveled to our school daily," said Mrs. Hortense Merritt, principal of The Ralph Bunche School.[3] Mrs. Merritt was also Superintendent of Sunday School at Calvary Baptist Church in Jamaica, NY where I was a Sunday School teacher.

Since P.S. 95Q only went to the fifth grade, my daughter was enrolled in our neighborhood school, IS 59Q. It wasn't long before rumors began to spread about an intermediate school being built in our community for white children only. There were meetings everywhere. I attended one of these meetings and couldn't find a parking space because there were so many vehicles. There were even buses bringing senior citizens, some with minor to moderate disabilities, to champion the cause for those who would benefit from the school. Inside the overcrowded auditorium, participants had begun making prepared speeches. These speakers, those for the all-white school and those against it, aroused the crowd. That night, I learned a lot about community involvement that would guide me in the future.

I.S. 231Q is located in Springfield Gardens, Queens. The school opened on September 19, 1977 with 500 hundred students.

But the departure of white students left its student body virtually all Black, and within months Black residents from neighboring Laurelton filed a complaint with the Federal Office of Civil Rights.

The agency ruled that the September 1977 creation of the annex, I.S. 238Q located at the corner of Merrick Boulevard and Cross Island Parkway had segregated the main building (I.S. 231Q) and warned that, unless action was taken to reverse this, New York City schools would lose federal funds. I.S. 238Q was closed on January 30, 1981. My worries were over when my daughter, April, was accepted to Hunter College High School in Manhattan. It was not, however, the hoped for Hunter College High School of Queens that Mrs. McCreary had envisioned.

CANADA, PUERTO RICO, AND ST. THOMAS

When April, was four years old, my husband and I wanted to begin exposing her to the culture of other countries. Canada was selected first because of its proximity to New York. We drove and made numerous stops along the way such as Harvard University in Boston, Massachusetts and Niagara Falls, upstate New York. While in Canada, we found that communicating with French-speaking Canadians was not as difficult as we had thought.

Later we took April to Puerto Rico at the advice of a neighbor who was purported to be a travel agent. April got A's on her report card in Spanish but was reluctant to put her knowledge into practice. When we heard that day trips were available, we decided to take a trip by plane to St. Thomas, U.S. Virgin Islands.

Upon our arrival in St. Thomas, we saw many vendors on the streets in Charlotte Amalie, along the shores of the Caribbean Sea.

That city is the principal business area because cruise ships from all over the world dock there. St. Thomas depends heavily on tourism, and businesses operate around the arrival and departure of the cruise ships. Observing the lights of the ships at night is a dramatic experience. The lights which can be seen beyond the Caribbean Sea make mountainside homes in the distance appear like a giant Christmas tree.

CHAPTER 18

Brazil 2007

I HAD LONGED TO VISIT Brazil, the country outside of Mother Africa with the largest population of African descendants, the majority of whom live in the city of Salvador. I decided to visit Salvador during the 2007 Mardi Gras. What I did not know was that the city would be on lockdown. No cars, buses, or taxis were allowed in the area where my hotel was located. Luckily, the taxi driver who spoke Portuguese, the native language, was able to reach the hotel without incident. Cloistered as I was, I managed to walk a few blocks where I witnessed poverty everywhere.

Along with other guests, I watched the carnival's parade from the balcony of the hotel. Tightly knitted throngs passed below following endless numbers of three-tiered flotillas. Policemen monitored the crowd in groups of four and kept good control of revelers. I couldn't believe my eyes when I saw the "wave" being performed by such a large number of people despite the high crime rate. The "wave" is usually performed at sports events by fans in the stadium that stand, arms raised, and sway from side to side in unison.

A few days later in Rio de Janeiro, a few feet from my hotel, I was the victim of an attempted robbery. As I walked at noon, in full view of many people, a young man riding a bicycle approached me from behind, grabbed my sapphire necklace, pulling it as he continued to pedal. The gold chain did not break. When I related the incident to other tourists in the hotel, one man said, holding out his wrist, "It happens all the time. I wear this bracelet from a box of corn flakes." I couldn't stop laughing.

From where I stood on Copacabana Beach, across the street from my hotel, in the horizon, I could see houses that seemed to cling precariously to the steep hillsides. These were favelas, or shanty towns, where poor people lived. Many of these people suffered from diseases because of overcrowding and the lack of proper infrastructure. These makeshift structures were made from wood scraps, eventually progressing to bricks, cinder blocks, and sheet metal. The view was in sharp contrast to the beautiful Christmas tree effect I had seen in St. Thomas.

CHAPTER 19

Eminent Domain
Demolishes Our Home

I WAS DISTRACTED FROM MY newly-established real estate business when I received a distress letter dated April 27, 1976 from my uncle, Rev. Weaver (Uncle Bubba), informing me that The City of Emporia was attempting to take our family property located at 115 South Main Street. Enclosed in his correspondence was a letter dated April 16, 1976 from the City's attorney stating, "I point out that we have been negotiating with members of your family in good faith for almost a year. We are no further along now than we were 10 months ago [approximately June, 1975]"

Soon thereafter on July 19, 1977, the City of Emporia exercised its right of eminent domain under Virginia code Ann.515.1-14 (Repl. 1973). Reason given, "for the purpose of construction and maintaining a public park within the City of Emporia. Description of property: ...said property being bounded on the west by South Main Street, on the south by Shiloh Street, on the east by lands formerly belonging to Jeff Walker and presently owned by the City of Emporia; and on the north by property owned by the United States of America and used for the United States Post Office, and said property fronting 37.50 feet on South Main Street, running back between parallel lines to property presently owned by the City of Emporia, Virginia."

The property described was conveyed to Walter H. Weaver, my grandfather, on February 2, 1904 and recorded in Deed Book 24, page 636 which indicates that the Weaver family had been in possession of this property for 72 years until the petition for eminent domain was signed. My grandfather's six children and three of his grandchildren, including me, were born and raised on that property at 115 South Main Street. Mama, Uncle Tom and Aunt Terris, his wife were the only family members living there. Eminent domain, not unlike lightning, struck the Weaver family with devastating consequences. Where would the family live? Could they relocate their businesses? How would Uncle Tom continue to pay for his two children's college tuition? And, how would the profit from the sale of the house be distributed among the five remaining heirs? Uncle Tom would not live to find out. He succumbed to a massive cerebral hemorrhage on January 24, 1976 when he found out that life, as he knew it, would never be the same.

Uncle Bubba, didn't like the low appraisal that was submitted by the state appraiser, and he wasn't happy with the lawyer-friend of the family. He retained a second lawyer and got them to agree and sign a contract stating that they would be co-counselors. All of the heirs had to sign a written agreement.

Needless to say, the Independent-Messenger, Emporia's bi-weekly newspaper had a field day. "Women Fault City on Relocation," "I'm Sure Race Has Something to Do With It" and "Women Upset Over Ouster" were some of their attention-getting headlines. And so our cherished home, the symbol of Weaver resilience and the holder of 72 years of priceless memories—family and fellowship, births and deaths, struggles and victories—was demolished to make way for a public park in Emporia.

CHAPTER 20

Islands in the Sun

As TIME WENT ON, I traveled to Antigua; Nassau, Bahamas; St. Kitts, Acapulco, Mexico; St. Croix and Tortola, British Virgin Islands; Trinidad and Tobago, and St. John in the U.S. Virgin Islands. During my day trip to Tortola, I was informed that Virgin Gorda, a nearby island was a must-see. I took a safari taxi to what turned out to be a cave created by volcanic activity years earlier. Descending down into the cave via a stairway, I witnessed what is referred to as "The Bath." This small, picturesque cave looked as if an above ground beach had been transplanted underground. Interestingly, vendors were there selling their wares.

I discovered St. John when friends in St. Thomas invited me to a picnic at Trunk Bay Beach, the most beautiful and most visited beach on St. John. After the picnic, we were invited to the home of a ferry boat owner who was a Black St. Johnian. I was impressed by his humility and business acumen. I later learned that Black St. Johnians owned most of the land on the island and that two historical dates were important to them: The 1733 Forstberg Slave Revolt and March 31, 1917, Transfer Day, when the Danish West Indies were formally ceded to the United States by Denmark in exchange for $25 million.

Not everyone was thrilled about the transfer. "There was weeping gnashing of teeth at the prospect of joining a nation that was noted for lynching as well as general mistreatment of its Black citizens. Also, the United States was involved in World War I which became a military government imposed on the islands," wrote Chuck Pishko in his newspaper column, "Remembrance of Transfer Day." He credits a 2011 article by Susan Lugo for the quote.[4] "...the Vessup Estate (Maho Bay) ruins are noteworthy as a representative building of the early settlement period in St. John and as the site of the rebel headquarters during the famous slave uprising of 1733..." (According to the Virgin Islands National Park's documents) "are now being renovated by a descendant of Harvey Monroe Marsh."[5] At one time I was in contract to purchase a parcel of land on Bourdeau Mountain being sold by another member of the Marsh family. When that did not materialize, I purchased property in Estate Chocolate Hole from a member of the Massack family.

St. John is a magnet for the rich and famous throughout the world, and I take notice when they purchase property in Estate Chocolate Hole. Kenny Chesney, a famous country music singer, and actress Renée Zellweger, were wed at Peter Bay and honeymooned at a villa in Estate Chocolate Hole. Tom Oates, a columnist and former editor of The St. John Tradewinds, recalled that Chesney incorporated island-themed songs in some of his work, such as the 2005 album, "Be As You Are," and "No Where To Go, Nowhere To Be."[6] He also wrote a song, "Hot Sauce Charlie" about a local musician named Trinidad Charlie.

CHAPTER 21

Paying Homage to
A Fallen Hero

WHEN I ARRIVED IN ATLANTA, Georgia, I was astonished to discover how far the airport was from residential dwellings, unlike JFK Airport in my hometown in Queens, New York where it is nestled within the community and a few feet from Jamaica Bay. Turning on the television in my hotel room is the first order of business when I travel. While unpacking, I heard a broadcaster announce, "There has been a massive Blackout in New York City." It was August 14, 2003 and the heat was oppressive. Normally, I would have been quite concerned. But somehow that day I was so happy to be away from home that I forgot about food that might spoil in my freezer in the absence of electricity. When I got settled, the concierge suggested I rent a car to visit places of interest but I declined for two reasons. First, I would be so engrossed in the process of driving in unfamiliar territory that I would not be fully able to appreciate my surroundings. Secondly, I would not be able to rub shoulders with the people of Georgia with whom I wanted to be up close and personal.

I made a pilgrimage to the Martin Luther King, Jr. National Historic Site and Museum, as well as Ebenezer Baptist Church. The area, once a moderate income community, had deteriorated. Yet, tourists from all over the world stood in line with me to experience the aura of this great man whose influence reverberated worldwide. I was glad I was there.

Traveling by bus and subway, I had the chance to meet many people who had migrated to Atlanta from the North. One was a woman who seemed to be an official greeter. She gave me instructions on how to reach Stone Mountain. After looking out the window for a while, I decided to speak to a man whom I assumed was on his way to work. He told me that buses did not travel all the way to the monument. If you didn't have a car, you had to walk.

Eventually, the bus came to my stop. Unfortunately, the bright sunny day did not decrease my fear of the long walk through this isolated, residential community. Finally, two young couples came along and I was glad for their presence. When we got there, it began to rain. Later, after walking with the young couples, I went to dine in a popular colonial-style restaurant that was founded by a slave woman. The food was delicious and exquisitely prepared and the ambiance, delightful. It was truly an eventful day.

CHAPTER 22

Saying Goodbye to Rosa Parks

ON OCTOBER 29, 2005, I was in Washington, DC attending a genealogical conference at Gallaudet University, a school offering education and career development for deaf and hard of hearing students. Suddenly I realized that after a memorial service in her home church in Montgomery, Alabama, Rosa Park's body would be transported to the Capitol Rotunda. I called my niece, Renee, and asked her to take me to the train station so that I could re-schedule my return to New York. I was not going to miss this op-portunity to pay my last respects to the "Mother of the Civil Rights Movement" in the 20th century, a woman who had been awarded the Congressional Gold Medal by President Bill Clinton.

After securing my luggage in the locker room and updating my train ticket, I spent a couple of hours exploring Union Station. Renee, who had lived in DC all of her life, said that she had never been inside the train station. It is comprised of two levels with escalators and elevators, several restaurants, and boutiques usu-ally found in shopping malls. I bought a pair of comfortable shoes because I didn't know how long I would have to stand in the procession.

A short walk through the park took me to the Capitol. It was about one o'clock in the afternoon and I was one of the first to arrive. Seven hours later, the body of Rosa Parks was placed in the Rotunda where I and thousands of other mourners formed a solemn procession around her casket. It was a very moving experience to be there and to realize that this woman, through her defiance of unjust laws, and her strong faith in God, set in motion actions that not only positively impacted the lives of Blacks in the United States, but changed the course of American history.

CHAPTER 23

The African Burial
Ground Memorial

SOUTH STREET FERRY WAS THE last stop on this subway train. Everyone seemed to know exactly where they were going. That is, everyone except me. It was Friday, October 5, 2007. The weekend passengers streamed out of the train and, like a huge tributary, emptied out to a rush of passengers from at least two other trains. Exits from the train led directly into Battery Park, which is located at the southern tip of Manhattan Island facing New York Harbor, the place where many immigrants and African slaves entered the United States.

New Yorkers, as well as tourists, meandered through the park enjoying the view of the harbor, the aesthetics of the park, and the crispness of the evening. Castle Clinton, located near the water's edge, was designated as the meeting place for those participating in the candlelight procession taking place that day. From there, all attendees began to walk solemnly towards the corner of Duane and Elk Streets carrying lit candles, as policemen on horses and motorcycles rode alongside us as escorts. The procession ended when we joined others who were engaged in another part of the memorial dedication. The purpose of the memorial was to honor slaves and other Blacks who had been buried centuries ago in lower Manhattan, before the sprawling city expanded above their graves.

CHAPTER 24

Two Floods: Countless Cries for Help

THE MISSISSIPPI RIVER, THE LONGEST river in North America, traverses Missouri, Illinois, Iowa, Wisconsin, Arkansas, Tennessee, Mississippi, and Louisiana. It flows downward to the Mississippi Delta, leaving at times devastation along the Gulf Coast states. August 23, 2005 was no exception as Hurricane Katrina slammed into the Gulf Coast states causing catastrophic damage and loss of life. The city of New Orleans was the hardest hit, sustaining more damage than other cities because its residents, the majority of whom were African Americans, were living in compromised communities. To add insult to injury, slow and inadequate response by local and state governments, the Federal Emergency Management Administration (FEMA), and the American Red Cross, left people drowning or hanging desperately from the roofs of their houses.

Author John M. Barry describes a more horrific flood in *Rising Tide: The Great Mississippi Flood of 1927 and How It Changed America*. Newspaper articles of events germane to the flood was his primary source of information. Defective construction of levees by the US Army Corps of Engineers was believed to be the responsible agent. When the levees broke and sandbags could not stop the flood waters, African-American men were forced, at gunpoint, to use their bodies as barricades against the rushing flood waters. Hundreds perished. In addition to this horror, African-American women, children, and men were forced onto muddy levees with herds of livestock. Militias formed by white planters, local and state officials, and National Guardsmen wielded guns to prevent African Americans from leaving the levees. The premise was that if the people "escaped" there would be no one to work on the farms and plantations.[7]

Hurricane Katrina victims can thank God that they weren't around during the 1927 flood. Yet, they didn't fare too much better. Victims of Hurricane Katrina were housed at the Louisiana Superdome (now the Mercedes-Benz Superdome), home of the New Orleans Saints football team. Soon filthy and squalor conditions developed due to overcrowding and lack of sanitation. Eventually, safety became a major issue as conditions became intolerable. Here, too, guns were used to prevent African Americans from crossing the Danziger Bridge to higher ground. There, two unarmed African Americans were gunned down and killed by members of the New Orleans Police Department, and four other African Americans were wounded. This was indeed a tragedy that compounded the devastation of the storm and the atrocities the people had already suffered.

Members of the Millions More Movement had made plans for a march on the nation's Capitol prior to Hurricane Katrina. I had missed attending previous events and was determined to attend the upcoming march. I boarded a chartered bus on October 15, 2005 along with others, to be a part of this historic undertaking. In Washington, I saw hundreds of young couples with their children walking around, while others sat on the grass with picnic baskets. The atmosphere was calm and serene. March organizers urged attendees to return home and help victims (often called "refugees" by the media) of Katrina that had been relocated. Soon after I returned from the Capitol, I was fortunate to meet a husband and wife team who shared my philosophy and desire for activism. We began to attend Millions More meetings under the direction of Bob Law, a national radio show host who was known for his activism in downstate New York. Meeting places changed from time to time with no reason given to the membership. Sometimes they were held at Abyssinian Baptist Church, Riverside Church, and Mosque #7, all located in New York City.

Although several issues were on the agenda, my friend Linda Bishop and I chose to become involved with Hurricane Katrina victims in Queens and Brooklyn. During these meetings, Bob Law devoted equal time, if not more, to the issue of the relationship between gun violence in the community and the video game, Grand Theft Auto. He organized a group to boycott several video stores in 2005 and appeared on ABC's television program "Like It Is" with legendary host Gil Noble (now deceased) several times expressing the urgent need for intervention.

It took eight years and at least five mass massacres in white communities before the nation awoke from her stupor. When radio and television broadcasters and politicians began to talk about violent video games and the need to ban them, the gaming industry blamed gun use as the culprit. Since then, the National Rifle Association (NRA), through its lobbyists in Congress, has been blocking numerous gun control measures, creating an impasse.

CHAPTER 25

Community Activism: Voter Registration

EVERY SUCCESSFUL POLITICAL CAMPAIGN HAS at its core a large base of eligible registered voters. I was particularly interested in the 2008 presidential election since the Democrats had for the first time an African-American candidate, Barack Obama, who appeared to be a strong contender. I was, however, unable to locate any Democratic Party organization in Queens in 2007 who was gearing up for the election. Despite all the excitement about the upcoming 2008 presidential election, there were no postings of meetings. When the opportunity came to join a group in Manhattan to travel by bus to register voters in Philadelphia for two days, I jumped at it without hesitation. That would be the first of many trips to Philadelphia. Eventually, a concerned citizen offered his office for meetings in Southeast Queens. Despite our efforts, we were informed by those representing the Democratic Party in the Manhattan headquarters that we would not receive funding because Pennsylvania and other battleground states needed the funds.

Most of those gathered for the first meeting seemed to have known each other, having been previously involved in local political election campaigns. The only experience I had was campaigning for Rev. Al Sharpton in his bid for the United States Senate in 1994. At that time, I became painfully aware of the campaign's need for funding. I offered my real estate office, free of charge, to a small number of volunteers for meetings. To raise funds, I suggested raffles and buttons with Rev. Sharpton's embossed photograph on them and advanced the money. At one meeting, a volunteer brought a friend with her. This newcomer stood up and questioned me about money that was being collected. It appeared that he had preconceived opinions before he came. I was apoplectic. Here I was doing most of the work and a spy had entered the camp. Since then, and until now, this "volunteer" was and still is a political operative. Having had that experience, I was leery of spies infiltrating our office as we worked on the campaign to elect a democratic president. Not to be discouraged, however, I kept my eyes on the prize.

We widened our voter registration area to include St. Albans, Cambria Heights, Springfield Gardens, Rosedale, Laurelton and parts of Jamaica. My friend Linda Bishop and I joined forces with a volunteer who represented a local civic organization to set up registration sites in front of the US Post Offices in the above-mentioned towns in order to reach the greatest number of people. When Barack Obama was elected president, we were all thrilled that we played at least a small part in his election.

CAMPAIGN 2011, FOR 2012 ELECTION

While vacationing in the South Pacific in February 2011, I was constantly thinking about the 2012 presidential election. This time the stakes were higher because members of the Republican Party had pledged to make President Barack Obama a one-term president at any cost. Fortified with experience gained from the 2008 campaign, I armed myself with personalized business cards which included Board of Election Offices, address, telephone numbers, and websites. I made hundreds of copies of fliers and pamphlets which I had designed and distributed earlier in the year. They included "Voters Need to Know the Truth," "What You Should Know About the Opponent," "Be Prepared: Photo License and ID Cards," and "National, State, and Local Elected Offices" (See Appendices 3 and 4). The latter included a diagram showing how local, state, and federal offices of government influenced what a president could or could not do. One of Linda's friends suggested that we could register more people and would not have to move from place to place if we set up our registration tables at the corner of Jamaica Avenue and 160ᵗʰ Street in Jamaica, Queens. She knew this because she worked in the Social Security building there.

Scaffolding around the building at Jamaica Avenue and 160ᵗʰ Street protected us from inclement weather from May 2011 until October 12, 2011, the deadline for registration. With the exception of having to pay for garage space and the absence of bathroom facilities, we were quite content with the location. There was constant pedestrian traffic representing people from all over the world. We were amazed to discover that so many people could not remember their last address, until we realized that some had been homeless. That was another problem to be addressed. Some senior citizens registered for the first time in their lives. Without being asked, one man came to the table and said, "I never voted because I don't want to serve on jury duty." We couldn't persuade him to change his mind. Many young African-American males said that they had felony convictions and could not vote. On the other hand, there were mothers who bought their 18-year-old children to register, others took forms home for members of their households; there were spouses who could not register but said, "I want to take a form home for my wife," or "I want to take this home to my husband." It was exciting when new citizens came smiling because they had waited so long for the opportunity to register and vote. Another joyous moment occurred when we decided it would be a good idea to post a large sign in Spanish as had been done in English. Many Spanish-speaking pedestrians took a second look and I could tell that they were pleased. Most of them completed the English language registration form. We registered 2,200 citizens. We were ably assisted by Queens residents Terri Hall of Jamaica, and Lisa Phillips of Cambria Heights.

After all the excitement and hard work involved in the re-election campaign was over, I was left with a moderate amount of inventory because I miscalculated the number of Obama tee-shirts needed. There were hardly any requests for small sizes in contrast to the high demand for extra large sizes. It was a lesson learned. "What are you going to do with these shirts?" I asked myself. Eureka! Out of the blue a thought came to me. How about giving them to some of the children you met in Ghana two years ago? I picked up the telephone and called Dr. Beryl Dorsett, an educator who previously served as the Assistant Secretary of Education in Washington, DC during the Reagan presidency in1987 and who is CEO of Africa Group World Traveller. I expressed my desire to donate the shirts and she informed me that she had planned a January 29, 2013 celebration in Ghana to commemorate the 2012 re-election of President Barack H. Obama. It could not have been a more fitting gift. As promised, Dr. Dorsett presented the 2012 Obama tee-shirts to the Sankofa Mbrofa Fie Children Culture Troupe based in Elmina, Ghana.

CHAPTER 26

Mining in the United States and Africa

AS A HEALTH PROFESSIONAL, I was curious as to what forces impacted the health of people in certain states, especially out West, and even outside of the United States. Mining was certainly one of them, as workers went deep into the belly of the earth to excavate natural resources like coal, copper, or other ores. Having earned a Master's Degree in Community Health, I became acutely aware not only how industrial conditions can adversely impact people, but also how they affect the environment as well. With this in mind, I set out to visit some of these mines in the U.S. and in Ghana.

Two of the sites I mention here were not included in my itineraries. They are coal mines in the Shawnee National Park in Southern Illinois, and platinum, diamond, gold and coal mines in South Africa. *Reckoning at Eagle Creek* by Jeff Biggers describes a century of weak laws regulating strip mining of coal and protection against environmental devastation on his family's homestead.[8] South Africa, the world's largest producer of platinum, ranks fifth in gold production with almost 50% of the world's gold reserve; it is the world's leader in diamond production and is the largest exporter of coal.

The AngloGold Ashanti Gold Mine in Obuasi, Ghana was closed on Easter Sunday, limiting our access to facilities at the mine. However, we were allowed to don workmen uniforms, headgear, and heavy boots and walk into the cavernous entrance of the mine. The AngloGold Ashanti Gold Mine is a global company with 21 subsidiary operations including The Cripple Creek and Victor subsidiaries located in the US with headquarters in South Africa.[9]

The Bingham Canyon Mine, also known as the Kennecott Copper Mine, is an open-pit mining operation extracting a large copper deposit southwest of Salt Lake City, Utah in the Oquirrh Mountains. The mine is owned by the Rio Tinto Group, an international mining and exploration company headquartered in the United Kingdom. The copper operations are managed through Kennecott Utah Copper Corporation. The open-pit mine is over 0.6 miles deep, 2.5 miles wide, and covers 1,900 acres. It was designated a National Historic Landmark in 1966.

Bingham Canyon had been one of the world's most productive mine up to 2004. At that time it produced more than 17 million tons of copper, 23 million ounces of gold, 190 million ounces of silver, and 850 pounds of molybdenum.[10] Since then, Arizona and New Mexico have surpassed it in production. The largest non-volcanic landslide in the history of North America occurred on April 10, 2013 at the Bingham Canyon Mine. A second slide occurred on September 11, 2013.

UTAH

I traveled to Salt Lake City, Utah, home of the Mormon Tabernacle Temple and Choir, to attend an annual conference convened by the genealogy society of which I am a member. My hotel was located on Temple Square. "How cool is this," I thought to myself. The highlight of the conference was doing genealogy research at The Family History Library of the Church of Latter-Day Saints. My paternal grandmother divorced my grandfather before I was born and never mentioned anything about his family. When I located their marriage license, I saw the names of his parents, my paternal great grandparents for the very first time!

Strolling along Temple Square in 2006 I did not see any African Americans. However, I did see two or three Native Americans who were wearing colorful shawls over modern clothing. Utah is home to five Native American tribes—the Ute, Goshute, Paiute, Navajo, and Shoshone.

I thought that there should have been more Native Americans there in the West because between 1830-1838 they had been forced from their homeland in the southeastern states, and made to walk to the New Territory, west of the Mississippi, known as "The Trail of Tears."

CHAPTER 27

Embracing the Motherland

ARMED WITH ANTI-MALARIA PILLS, INSECT repellent, and hearts filled with compassion, members of my travel group boarded Delta Airlines Flight 166 from JFK Airport in New York on March 29, 2010. We landed in Accra, Ghana eleven hours later. This trip to West Africa would be unlike previous trips where everything was fun and relaxation. This was a working trip and our mission was to render medical and other services to adults and children in various rural villages.

Several nurses in the group, including me, took blood pressure readings under a large tree while long lines of villagers stood in the sweltering 104° heat. Others in the group, mostly school teachers, taught and gave demonstrations to school children and adults. In addition to rendering our services, each of us brought donations of medical or school supplies for the people. We traveled by bus to rural districts where there were no stores or restaurants, so I was surprised when our guide yelled, "Does anyone want to make a 'bush stop?'" It was only then that I realized our bus did not have a bathroom and why we were advised to bring toilet paper.

The following day, we visited two handicraft shops and a plantation. In the village of Bonwire, we observed men design and weave yarn on oversized looms to create what is known as kente cloth. In the nearby village of Ahwiaa, we were bombarded by aggressive vendors who tried to get us to buy woodcarvings. Like slick Madison Avenue ad men, each touted the value of their product, yet they were all selling identical carvings. At the end of the day, we explored Sewfi Cocoa Plantation in the Western Region where we plucked pods from trees that contained cacao seeds that, after a drying process, became what we call chocolate and cocoa.

Early one morning, our group entered the grounds of Cape Coast Slave Dungeon. We were all thinking about Sankofa and "The Door of No Return." It is said that when Africans were chained and dragged through the door of the dungeon onto slave ships they would never return to Africa. But we, their descendants, did return. The interior of the dungeon was dark and damp, the floor was still covered with cobblestones as it was centuries ago.

Our next stop was a visit to Seestah Imahkus' establishment, One Africa, which is a restaurant and tour service enterprise located in the district of Elmina on Cape Coast. I recalled having seen CNN television anchor Anderson Cooper's documentary of One Africa sometime before. Unlike the yellow brick road in the Wizard of Oz movie, the soil in Ghana appears to be orange. Huts in the villages are made from clay, reinforced with tree branches or bamboo for support. As we entered the compound of One Africa, we felt cool breezes coming off the nearby Gulf of Guinea and heard water splashing against shoreline rocks surrounding part of the compound. To our left was a picturesque semi-circle of orange-colored, detached hut-shaped guest houses with thatched roofs. A sprawling outdoor restaurant was the centerpiece of the compound.

Seestah Imahkus is the author of *Returning Home Ain't Easy But It Sure Is A Blessing*, her autobiography. A native New Yorker, she describes the joys and trials of relocating to Africa. She is concerned that some changes to Cape Coast Slave Dungeon is an attempt to erase an important part of history. The assertion that 27 of approximately 60 slave-holding and related facilities were along the coast of Ghana was no surprise to me. However, I was somewhat surprised to learn that there were designated villages where white "slavers" kept the African women with whom they cohabitated and produced children.

It was our last night in Ghana, and there had not been enough time to shop for souvenirs other than kente cloth, wood carvings, and cheap trinkets. I stole away from the group during their sorority farewell ritual and spoke to the man in charge of wrapping and shipping our purchases. I expressed my situation to him and he directed me to one of our tour guide's assistants who traveled with us. Pointing, he said, "That young man lives in this area and he knows where to take you." I recognized the young man and he agreed to take me to purchase souvenirs.

When we took a taxi, I began to have second thoughts. It was a moonless night, there were no lights on the highway, and we drove for what seemed like hours. I asked repeatedly, "Are we there yet?" Finally, we arrived at what appeared to be a roadside tent-city, closed for the night. I touched my gold earrings, bangles, and necklace as we walked closer to the entrance, and to my dismay I realized I was dressed inappropriately for this venture. I was wearing a beautiful red, long, form-fitting African style dress. Again, my escort reassured me that I would be safe (I was nervous because he was of small stature).

Entering the warehouse, I observed a woman and a small child in a crib-like structure covered with mosquito netting. As we advanced through the corridor, we were approached by a man who seemed to be in command. Suddenly, men approached us out of the darkness. I began to retreat. Again, I was reassured by my escort and the man in charge. I purchased beautiful, well-made souvenirs for my friends and returned safely to the hotel unharmed.

CHAPTER 28

South Africa: Home of President Nelson Mandela

SOUTH AFRICAN AIRWAYS FLIGHT 204 left JFK Airport in Queens, NY on March 27, 2008 headed for Johannesburg, South Africa with a two-hour layover in Dakar, Senegal where security personnel searched only one section of the plane. I was impressed by the beautiful dresses and head wraps worn by the women boarding the plane. We landed at the International Airport in Johannesburg after 17 hours and 25 minutes flight time, anxious to reconnect to our motherland.

Everyone in our tour group was well aware of South Africa's apartheid policies and history of abuse. When it was dismantled, Africans of all ethnicities were allowed to vote in the first democratic election. That same year, 1994, Nelson Rolihlahla Mandela became president of South Africa after being imprisoned for 27 years.

In Johannesburg, our first stop was in Soweto, the township known for its overcrowded population and decadent infrastructure. On a happier note, walking through the former home of Nelson Mandela was a cheerful experience. This is where he had lived, at separate times, with his first and second wives and their families. Just up the street from there, was the home of Bishop Desmond Tutu, another fearless social activist and Nobel Prize winner.

While many countries in Africa claim to be the original cradle of civilization, I will leave that for the archeologists to decide. Nevertheless, South Africa has a tourist attraction known as the Cradle of Humanity which is located an hour's drive from Johannesburg. The Cradle of Humanity is an integral part of the Sterkfontein, a series of limestone caves where anthropological digs have yielded fossils which date back more than four million years.

Our next stop was the Letamo Game Farm. It was quite a distance northwest of Johannesburg, and several species of wild animals roamed freely. Fortunately, we were traveling in a bus. We arrived safely at the Cradle of Roots Restaurant at Forum Homini, a low-lying architectural delight nestled in tropical flowers and foliage, overlooking what appeared to be a lake. Service was excellent and the food was delicious.

Strolling around the front of the restaurant after dinner, we observed couples and families walking down a descending pathway into what appeared to be an underground structure. Sandra, my roommate, queried, "Where are they going?" Looking bewildered, I replied, "I have no idea, there is no mention of this in the itinerary." Later, we found out that the underground structure was Forum Homini Boutique Hotel, a series of cave apartments. I still cannot get over the fact that people would bring their children from all over the world to vacation in caves.

We boarded another airplane and landed in Cape Town, known to travelers as the most beautiful city in the world. Indeed, it is very beautiful if one can ignore the high razor-blade fences around houses in the white communities. Cape Town's Victoria & Alfred

Waterfront and the Nelson Mandela Gateway to Robben Island, a World Heritage Site, is where we boarded a ferry to tour the prison and stand next to the cell where Nelson Mandela had been imprisoned. Outside we saw piles of rock quarried by Mandela and left there as a reminder of his ordeal.

Returning to Victoria & Alfred Waterfront again for lunch, we got a wonderful surprise. There was actress Sheryl Lee Ralph walking towards us. Although we didn't know her personally, we greeted each other affectionately. Since appearing in the original cast of *Dream Girls* years ago, she has been active in various civic and humanitarian causes. She was in South Africa primarily, on behalf of The Sister's Circle, an annual four-day summit to bring together both African and African-American women infected with HIV-AIDS to share their stories and plan a course of action. She is a spokesperson for the Names Foundation Campaign for AIDS entitled *Call My Name*. This initiative involves traveling throughout the country in an attempt to call attention to the AIDS crisis and have African Americans add more panels to the National HIV-AIDS Memorial Quilts in honor of their loved ones who have succumbed to the disease.

This trip to South Africa turned out to be a special one in many ways. "Happy birthday, Ethel!" was the joyous greeting I heard from my fellow travelers as I entered Moyo at Stellenbosch Restaurant in Cape Town on April 2, 2008. Moyo, which is Swahili for "soul," is situated in an expansive garden where attractive tents and gazebos offer protection from the elements, while enhancing the beauty and decor of the restaurant. The atmosphere was festive as drummers went from table to table entertaining us. Later, they gave a stellar performance on stage. It was a birthday I'll never forget!

Another flight, more immigration procedures, and another ferry ride took us to where the borders of Zambia, Zimbabwe, Namibia, and Botswana meet in the middle of the Zambezi River. According to the Zambia National Tourist Board, Zambia is bordered by Angola, Botswana, The Democratic Republic of Congo, Malawi, Mozambique, Namibia, Tanzania, and Zimbabwe on land.

From Kasane, Botswana, after yet another flight, more immigration protocol, and two ferry rides, we embarked on a picturesque and thrilling land and river safari. I would be remiss if I did not mention that baboons and monkeys roam around freely especially when food is available. Tourists are warned not to feed or pet them because they have been known to snatch food from your hands!

CHAPTER 29

Civil Disobedience for A Cause: Sean Bell Case

SEVEN YEARS AFTER AMADOU DIALLO of the Bronx was assassinated by police officers who fired 41 bullets into his body, another Black man was killed in a barrage of 50 bullets fired by police officers in Queens. Sean Bell was killed just hours before his wedding, and two of his friends Trent Benefeld and Joseph Guzman were severely wounded on November 25, 2006. Both Diallo and Bell were innocent. Most African Americans, including me, believe that racial profiling, an abhorrent policy practiced by New York City police officers, was at the root of this tragedy. I placed flowers at the site where Bell was shot. A few days later, I attended a mass rally in Lower Manhattan. On December 16, 2006, I was among the tens of thousands who marched in protest down Fifth Avenue in Manhattan.

The House of The Lord Church in Brooklyn, where Rev. Dr. Herbert Daughtry is the pastor, was the meeting place for a march across the Brooklyn Bridge. The bridge has an entrance on Atlantic Avenue. Rev. Al Sharpton and his contingency were to meet us on the Manhattan side of the bridge. As we neared the entrance to the Brooklyn Bridge, policemen on horseback tried to block our way. Those leading our contingency began to run, heading for the Williamsburg Bridge, and we followed. We were soon surrounded by other mounted police as well as those on foot. Those of us who had planned to practice civil disobedience sat down and waited to see what was going to happen. We were handcuffed, squeezed into a paddy-wagon and hauled off to the 84th Precinct in Lower Manhattan. While waiting to be photographed and fingerprinted, we could hear strains of familiar songs coming from the other side of the building where the men were being held. We soon recognized that they were singing "We Shall Overcome" and other freedom songs.

Five women occupied the jail cell with me, each of us refusing to use an open toilet which mockingly represented the oppressive justice system. We were offered stale peanut butter and jelly sandwiches which we refused. When we were released after approximately five to six hours, one woman took her sandwich with her as a souvenir. The date was May 7, 2008, two years after Sean Bell's murder and the acquittal of the officers involved in the shooting.

About this time, so as not to lose momentum, Rev. Al Sharpton, founder and president of National Action Network, planned and executed a demonstration around the Justice Department in Washington, DC. Like David in the Bible, we were up against a proverbial Goliath. But that did not deter us. We were coming against our giant "in the name of the Lord" (1Samuel 17:45). We were relying on our faith in God and the promises of the scriptures to see us through because "...faith is the substance of things hoped for, the evidence of things not seen," (Hebrews 11:1) and "By faith the walls of Jericho fell down, after they were compassed about seven days" (Hebrews 11:30). We knew that if we wanted to cast a national spotlight on the atrocities of police brutality against minorities and wanted the inequities in the justice system to change, we would have to launch a strategic plan of action and be persistent in our efforts. We would have to emulate the biblical Joshua and his men who "rose early about the dawning of the day, and compassed the city after the same manner seven times: only *on that day* (author's emphasis) they compassed the city seven times" (Joshua 6:15). This sustained movement was in pursuit of equal justice for African Americans and other minorities in the courts of the United States of America.

Civil rights activists of all ages and ethnicities, from across the country, converged on the Justice Department. We, too, "rose early about the dawning of the day." My friend Linda and I traveled from Queens to Harlem, where we boarded a bus at National Action Network's headquarters at four o'clock in the morning headed for Washington, DC. Many senior citizens participated, as did many who had physical disabilities.

Since passengers on tour buses are not permitted to disembark near historical sites in Washington, DC, we were routed to a designated parking area and traveled by subway to our destination. After a short walk, we came to an area known as the Federal Triangle. Located just north of the National Mall, it stretches from the White House to the Capitol Building, and houses several federal buildings. It is located between Pennsylvania and Constitution Avenues and Fifteenth Street, North West and is a part of the Pennsylvania Avenue National Historic Site. The Department of Justice building lies within the Federal Triangle bounded by Constitution and Pennsylvania Avenues and Ninth and Tenth Streets. Did the walls fall that day? No, but cracks began to appear in the administration's foundation. As Rev. Adam Clayton Powell, Jr., the Congressman, used to say when his people got weary of trying to fight City Hall, "Keep the faith!" ...and we did.

CHAPTER 30

International Sweethearts
of Rhythm

I REMEMBER THE SWEETHEARTS OF Rhythm, an all-girl band, staying in our home when they came to Emporia to perform at the Southern Club, owned by Mama and Uncle Tom. The official name of the band was International Sweethearts of Rhythm because they performed abroad as well as nationally. The band members were young, friendly and full of laughter. As a young girl, I was impressed with the way they styled their hair and the clothes they wore. They wore blouses and slacks while most of the women and girls in Emporia and Greensville County wore dresses and skirts. Sadly, in later years when I asked people from the South if they ever heard of the group, their reply was always, "No."

Imagine how ecstatic I was when I heard the words "Sweethearts of Rhythm" mentioned on C-Span 2 Book TV on July 22, 2006 in connection with a woman named Cathy L. Hughes who had received the Phillis Wheatley Award. Ms. Hughes was the daughter of one of the members of the International Sweethearts of Rhythm, Helen Jones Woods, a trombonist. I would like to think that her mother was one of the young ladies who spent the night at our house.

The band originated at Piney Woods Country Life School, a free boarding school for poor and orphaned Colored children in Mississippi. It was founded by Mr. Lawrence C. Jones. Students worked and were taught a trade. (A similar school existed in New Jersey during this period). Students who excelled in playing musical instruments became members of the band. The band existed from 1937-1955 with members joining and leaving from time to time.

Ms. Catherine "Cathy" Hughes is a board member at Piney Woods Country Life School. She is also co-founder of Radio One (1979), founder of TV One (1999), has owned numerous radio stations, is a member of the New York Stock Exchange, and is a minority owner of BET Industries.[11]

CHAPTER 31

From Deep Rivers to Wide Oceans

WHEN I WAS INVITED TO a wedding in Monroe, Louisiana, I accepted immediately knowing it would give me the opportunity to visit New Orleans, the city where Uncle Tom's wife, Terris Tassin, grew up. More importantly, I would see the great Mississippi River—as it flowed into the Gulf of Mexico where the Atlantic and Pacific Oceans meet. The ride on the Mississippi River Boat was the highlight of my trip. I was amazed to see that the River, its shores lined with tall oil rigs spouting flames into the air, was still a busy commercial highway with heavy-laden barges carrying hundreds of barrels and cases of products.

The scene reminded me of the Meherrin River and its journey through Emporia, Virginia, as it winds its way through North Carolina where it merges with the Chowan River, drains into the Albermarle Sound, throws itself wildly into the Atlantic Ocean, then joyfully meets the Pacific Ocean at the Gulf of Mexico.

Eight years after my first glimpse of the Pacific Ocean, I was finally going to the South Pacific: Australia, New Zealand, and the Fiji Islands. Flying time from New York and Los Angeles to

Brisbane, Australia was twenty-two hours and twenty minutes. At the airport, a small dog circled my carry-on luggage, sniffing it as security guards approached me. I had forgotten to indicate on my immigration form that I was in possession of a meat sandwich. They issued me a "You have breached Australian Quarantine Law" certificate but allowed me to enter. Our tour guide recounted how a tourist had been fined $500 for having an apple. I was not fined. Thank you, Australia. Next stop, New Zealand.

New Zealand is comprised of North Island and South Island located south of Australia, and is separated by the Tasman Sea. Situated on a volcanic plateau, it is prone to earthquakes and tsunamis such as the one in 2011, one year prior to our visit. Damages which were sustained in Christchurch prevented our tour group from going there.

Despite its problematic geological conditions, New Zealand, known as the "Paradise of the South Pacific," is beautiful. According to history, "Ancient Polynesians were settled in New Zealand before the first outsider, an American Negro, Andrew Power, survivor of a massacred European headhunting party, was brought captive into the Taupo area in 1813."[12]

In Rotorua, North Island volcanic activity was ever present. In the village of the Maori people we saw bubbling mud, geysers, and boiling lakes of all sizes. Interestingly, many of these steam holes were actually in the backyard of homes, and food was sometimes cooked in the boiling water. Children played nearby, unprotected, but without fear. The boiling lakes are not without merit since in at least one instance that we observed, electricity was being generated from the boiling water to supply a nearby hospital.

Arriving at Nadi International Airport in Fiji from Auckland, New Zealand, we boarded a bus that would take us to an exclusive, hideaway resort on the island of Yanuca. Our journey was bumpy as we traveled along dismally dark unpaved roads and crossed several unsteady bridges that had been damaged previously by earthquakes and torrential rains. It was Saturday night and people were casually walking along the side of the road, as if going to a party. Every now and then, far in the distance, we could see flickers of light dancing in the darkness. Nevertheless, by day, Fiji provided the sun, sand, and intimate haven we all desired. I was surprised to learn that the Indian population on the island (descendants from India) was almost as large as the native Fijians (51% Fijian, 44% Indian). During my limited stay, I observed many Indians as owners and managers while Fijians were their employees.

CHAPTER 32

Ground Zero, Cemeteries, and Monuments

"WE INTERRUPT THIS BROADCAST..." A voice on the radio cut abruptly through the regular morning banter to bring the following earth-shaking news: "There has been an attack on the World Trade Center." I had been listening in the medical room of the public school where I had been assigned. Without waiting for more, I jumped out of the chair and ran out of the building. I was joined by another employee whom I did not know. She had also been listening to a radio. Meanwhile, teachers in their classrooms had no idea what was happening. My colleague and I looked in the sky to determine if we, in Brooklyn, could see smoke billowing over Manhattan. We could. Back in the medical room, I continued to listen to details of what was happening that day—Tuesday, September 11, 2001.

Two years later, I had an appointment at 125 Barclay Street in Lower Manhattan. I decided not to drive because finding parking in Manhattan was extremely difficult. I never lived or worked in Manhattan, and went there only occasionally for shopping and special events. Traveling by subway, I had to change trains to reach the World Trade Center, my designated stop. As I stepped out of the train I realized that it was, among other things, a hub and major connection point for trains coming into Lower Manhattan. When I reached street level, I saw people rushing to and fro. I was in the heart of the financial district. Detour signs were posted everywhere, and heavy-duty tractors and equipment could be seen in large craters excavating soil from deep down inside the earth. To navigate all this activity, it took me twice as long to get to my appointment since one Manhattan block is the equivalent of three or four blocks elsewhere. 125 Barclay Street was only one block from Ground Zero.

When I returned home that evening, I had an epiphany. For the first time it hit me that I had actually been to Ground Zero. I began to feel somewhat guilty and remorseful. "Why did I have that mental block?" I asked myself. After much soul searching, ten years later I realized that it was a precursor to what I would discover in the cemetery where my ancestors were buried—sunken graves and the absence of grave markers.

Each Memorial Day, Mama took my sister Elsie and me to Cottage Cemetery to pay homage to the ancestors. We would clear the graves by pulling overgrown vines and cutting down weeds and saplings; afterwards we would decorate them by placing pretty home-grown flowers in mason jars. Over the years, I attended many burials there. In 2012, my cousin Stanley Carter and I journeyed to Emporia for the sole purpose of cleaning the grave sites. Before we arrived, Jeanette Kemp Thomas' daughter, Rev. Dr. Denise Avent, and her grandson, Jerry Thomas, had located the site (a few feet from their ancestors' plot) and cleaned half of the area. With the passing of time, the area had become densely overgrown. They surprised us with a custom-made signpost with "Weaver Family" printed on it. The Kemp and Weaver families who had lived next door to each other still maintained a very close relationship. Denise's aunt, Iris Kemp Woodward, had been my best friend. My paternal cousins, Pat Wilkins and Emmett Michael, assisted us with the clean-up.

As we were cleaning, I realized that I had not seen a grave marker for my grandfather, Walter Hamilton Weaver, Sr., who had died before I was born. I decided that the sunken space between his wife, Mamie L. Weaver and his oldest child, Elsie, was probably his resting place. When I contacted a company to make and install a vault top, I realized that I did not know the date of my grandfather's death.

I applied to the Commonwealth of Virginia, Department of Health for a Certificate of Death. The response was as follows:

May 3, 2013, "With exception of the years 1897 to June 1912, the Office of Vital Records has records of births and deaths since 1853. Vital Records has divorce records on file from 1918 to the present and marriage records from 1853 to the present. There are no records prior to 1853 and there was no law for the registration of births and death between 1897 and June 14, 1912: May 15, 2013, no record was found during the period of 1920-1949; and July 8, 2013, no record was found during the period of 1912 thru 1949."

It's almost inconceivable that there is no record of my grandfather's death. One would think that he never existed. My first cousin, Rev. Thomas Arnold Nance and I concluded, based on what our grandmother had told us, that our grandfather died in 1926 and that is what I had inscribed on his vault.

CHAPTER 33

Rewriting History

VISITING MY HOMETOWN IS VERY painful when I pass the U.S. Post Office's parking lot, where my family's home used to be. A few feet away stands the Richards Memorial Library where I went to search for information concerning the area. The librarian referred me to *Sketches of Greensville County, 1650-1967,* First Edition, 1968, a book sponsored by The Riparian Woman's Club of Emporia, Virginia. I purchased the book and was horrified to discover that African Americans were hardly mentioned, with the exception of Chapter XI: "The Negro in Greensville County," and Chapter XII, "A Tribute to Faithful Slaves." In Chapter XI it is alleged that Negro slaves were happy and content; that they were primitives from Africa accustomed to living in substandard conditions, and that they had simple desires. Moreover, they had nothing to worry about because they had free clothing, free food, and free housing. Most of all, they had compassionate masters. "They were bound to each other," the writer said. The last paragraph referenced two school principals, now deceased, who made enormous contributions in the field of education.

As I read that paragraph, I became aware that when others write your history, they tell it the way they want it to be perceived.

One of the principals was my own high school principal. Although he was one of the 65 foot soldiers that signed the NAACP's Charter on June 10, 1940, he could not be vociferous regarding civil rights and equal justice and keep his job as principal. I was there. Chapter XII, "A Tribute to Faithful Slaves," tells about two Negro slaves, Uncle Merrill and Uncle John, both of whom were brothers and were owned by the same master. They were traveling with the master and the master's family from Virginia to South Carolina during the Civil War, and for some unknown reason the master departed, and the brothers had to forage for food to feed everyone. When they returned to Virginia, Uncle Merrill was overwhelmed by "freedom" and unable to care for his own large family. Uncle John who had never married, had no children. When he died, he left his entire estate to the master's younger children. Apparently nothing for his nieces and nephews (the author's opinion).[13] There were so many omissions and gross neglect in the first edition, a second edition was published. For example, there was no mention of the two legendary restaurants, The Mid Way Café and the Dew Drop Inn, that were known near and far as places to use the bathrooms, sit down and enjoy a meal. This second edition was basically the same book with an extensive addendum, which was more inclusive.

Emporia, Virginia's newspaper, the Independent-Messenger, is delivered to my home in New York twice a week. After all these years away from home, I haven't broken the umbilical cord. Throughout 2008 and 2009, notices were published in the Independent-Messenger informing everyone that they had the opportunity of writing their own history. County Heritage, Inc. had published heritage books for other counties throughout the South. Many people who do not read the paper were not aware of this awesome opportunity. Using my Emporia telephone directory, I called everyone I knew and made copies of Chapter XI and Chapter XII, mailed them with a cover letter expressing the urgent need to participate. And they complied. *The Heritage of Greensville County, Virginia 1781-2009* was published in 2010 by The Greensville Co. Heritage Book Committee, County Heritage Inc., Publishers. I donated a copy of the book to The Library of Congress for use by writers, historians, and genealogists. I also donated a copy of *Greensville-Emporia NAACP, Celebrating a Heritage of Service and Sacrifice, June 10, 1940-June 23, 2007.* This extensive journal, too, contains valuable historical information. Upon receipt of the books, I received a letter from Bridgetta C. Jenkins, Head of The Monographs Section stating, "We are happy to inform you that each of these publications was selected for addition to the Library's General Collection, and each was assigned a Library of Congress control number (LCCN)."[14] These two books were also donated to the Schomburg Center for Research in Black Culture.

CHAPTER 34

Reconciliation

Young children are very sensitive to their surroundings, and as a child I was no different. I saw white children attending school in the big, brick building across from our house every day and I wondered why I couldn't attend. I was Black. I could not enter the armory across the street where they sometimes had entertainment. I was Black. The same held true for the Pitts Theatre, one block uptown where professional Blacks lined-up on the side of the building to sit in the balcony. Whites, on the other hand, entered through the front doors, and sat in the main section of the theatre where they could see very well. Friends sometimes do not understand why, even at this stage of my life, I do not frequent movie houses. It's called post traumatic stress.

Today, most children in Emporia attend public schools; others attend the all-white Brunswick Academy, including brown children of Asian doctors. The original Boys and Girls Club is housed in the armory and membership is predominantly African American. Overall, racial progress has been incremental. History, however, was made on December 30, 2012 in Emporia, when Mary L. Person was sworn in as mayor. She is the first woman to be elected, as well as, the first African American to hold the office. She was also the principal of Greensville County Elementary School and had previously served two years as Emporia City Council member.

Looking out at the sea of faces of her supporters during the swearing-in ceremony, Ms. Person said, "I'm overwhelmed and I'm so thankful that you're here to share this day with me. I look back on January 12, 1988, there was a consent decree entered by the United States District Court for the Eastern District of Virginia as a result of a civil action suit by Thomas M. Person and others against William H. Ligon and others. The decree established districts to be sued for electing the members of Council, determining on their own the number of members of Council to be elected in each district, and the terms of office for the members of Council. He was trying to make sure that we had equal representation on the Council."

One more wall in the racial divide had come tumbling down. Thomas Person was the mayor's father. His younger sisters and I attended school together. He and his sister Rose Person Allen were always helpful to me when I needed assistance with research projects.

In the summer of 2013, my cousin, Pat, invited me to a concert in the Meherrin River Park. I had to walk over the pavement in the United States Post Office parking lot where my family home once stood, to reach the main tent. I stood on, what was to me, sacred ground and looked upward towards heaven and said, "Mama, they really did make this a public park."

THE END

APPENDIX 1

Greensville – Emporia NAACP

Alphabetized Listing of Charter Members and Officers
(Submitted to National Office May 14, 1940; Approved June 10,
1940

Officers	Position	Occupation
Dr. F.A. Sealy	President	Dentist
Dr. W.D. Joyner	Vice President	Physician
Mrs. G.P. Waller	Secretary	Teacher
Dr. C.W. Cartwright	Treasurer	Physician

	Charter Members	Occupation
1.	Rev. Alexander B. Batts	Farmer
2.	Mr. Joseph C. Bond	Mortician
3.	Mrs. Nannie M. Boswell	Housewife
4.	Mr. David Bradley	Tinsmith
5.	Mr. William Butts	Farmer
6.	Mr. George Cain	Farmer

7.	Mr. R.C. Cain	Farmer
8.	Dr. C.W. Cartwright	Physician
9.	Mrs. Daisy S. Cartwright	Housewife
10.	Mr. Kenny Clark	Laborer
11.	Mrs. Martha Cooke	Beautician
12.	Mr. Willie Curley	Insurance Agent
13.	Mrs. Martha Davenport	Teacher
14.	Mr. Lemuel Davis	Truck
15.	Mr. Robert Davis	Laborer
16.	Mrs. Anna L. Ellis	Insurance Agent
17.	Mr. H.L. Flowers	Laborer
18.	Mr. Henry Gary	Farmer
19.	Mr. James Greene	Businessman
20.	Mr. Charlie High	Farmer
21.	Mr. Horace High	Farmer
22.	Atty. Oliver W. Hill	Attorney
23.	Mr. Walter Holmes	Farmer
24.	E.L. Jackson	Businessman
25.	Mr. T.Y. Jackson	Blacksmith
26.	Mr. Edward W. Jones	Taxi Owner
27.	Mrs. Oscar Jones (or James)	Fireman
28.	Mrs. Betty S. Joyner	Teacher
29.	Dr. W.D. Joyner	Physician
30.	Mr. John A. Knox	Teacher
31.	Mr. Joseph Lewis	Laborer
32.	Mr. John Lundy	Plumber

33.	Mr. E.D. Mason	Mortician
34.	Atty. Thurgood Marshall*	Attorney
35.	Mr. David Palmer	Farmer
36.	Mrs.Mamie Peebles/Peoples	Businessperson
37.	Rev. Simon A. Pelham	Minister
38.	Mr. Romnie T. Person	Masonry Contractor
39.	Mr. Isham Randolph	Farmer
40.	Atty. Leon A. Ransom	Attorney
41.	Mr. Henry Reese	Taxi Owner
42.	Mrs. Raphael Reese	Beautician
43.	Mr. Zack Ricks	Laborer
44.	Mr. Willie Roberts	Farmer
45.	Mr. G.W. Robinson	Businessman
46.	Mr. Willie Robinson	Blacksmith
47.	Dr. F.A. Sealy	Dentist
48.	Rev. E.D. Shands	Minister
49.	Mrs. Lillian Simmons	Business Owner
50.	Mr. Frank H. Smith	Principal/Teacher
51.	Rev. J.E. Spratley	Minister
52.	Mr. Sidney Stith	Laborer
53.	Mr. Stephen Thomas	Salesman
54.	Mr. Fred D. Thompson	Teacher
55.	Mrs. Agnes Walker	Housewife
56.	Mrs. Gertrude P. Waller	Teacher
57.	Rev. J.H. Waller	Minister/Teacher
58.	Miss Priscilla Waller	Beautician

59.	Mr. Thomas Weaver**	Barber
60.	Mr. Walter Weaver**	Barber
61.	Mr. Daniel Wilkins	Business Owner
62.	Mr. George C. Williams	Farmer
63.	Mr. George D. Williams	Extension Agent
64.	Mr. John M. Williams	Taxi Driver
65.	Mr. Henry Witherspoon	Farmer

* *Became U.S. Supreme Court Justice*

** Uncles of author

This list was discovered in the Library of Congress by Mr. Steve J. Ackerman, a journalist.

Types of Nursing Programs

LICENSED PRACTICAL NURSE PROGRAMS

NURSING SCHOOL PROGRAMS FOR LPNs are available through vocational-technical schools and community colleges. These are usually year-long programs that allow the graduate to apply for entry-level positions after passing a state licensing examination.

REGISTERED NURSE PROGRAMS
DIPLOMA PROGRAMS-HOSPITAL SCHOOLS OF NURSING

According to the National League for Nursing, fewer than 100 hospital-based programs are available today. Earning a diploma qualifies licensed graduates for entry-level RN positions. These programs are usually three years long. Graduates of the program receive a wealth of clinical experience unlike the degree programs.

ASSOCIATE DEGREE PROGRAMS (ADN)

ADN programs are offered through community and four-year colleges. An associate degree is equivalent to a hospital-based diploma in terms of education. These programs are usually two years long and prepare the graduate for entry-level positions. However, most employers are reluctant to hire these nurses until they acquire at least one year of practical hospital experience elsewhere.

Bachelor (Baccalaureate) of Science (BSN)

Bachelor of Science in Nursing degrees are offered in many four-year colleges. Students can enter as freshmen and nurses with ADN degrees and can advance their careers by matriculating at a 4-year college to earn a BSN. The BSN enables the nurse to work in a wider variety of professional roles and settings. As with the ADN graduate, most employers require at least one year of practical experience before they will hire the graduate.

Nursing Organizations

American Nurses Association (ANA)
National League for Nursing Accreditation Commission (NLNAC)
State Board of Nursing
National Council of State Boards of Nursing
American Student Nurses Association

What You Should Know About the Opponent

MEDIA OWNERS

FIRST, UNDERSTAND THAT A MONOPOLY exists when one or a few persons are allowed by Congress to own and operate several television networks, a considerable amount of radio stations, and multiple newspapers. That is the problem facing **President Obama** and the **Democratic Party** today.

Far right conservatives dominate the media because they own and control most of it. The media is their "bully pulpit" and they refuse to present fair and balanced information. Owners have colorful, combative, narcissistic sabre-toothed rattlers to do their dirty work. He/she is the host of various media programs. Other would-be hosts are impressed with the notoriety the lead host is receiving and begin to emulate him/her, at times being more ridiculous. They distort the facts and give false information.

Propaganda

Secondly, these talking heads follow the **exact script** given by the owners to the lead host and they parrot the **exact script** day in and day out trying to persuade the public. When President Obama was first elected, owners and talking heads went ballistic! **"Take Back Our Country!"** became the battle cry. Remember owners do not hesitate to fire a host if he/she does not follow the **exact script**.

Lead hosts and would-be hosts led their followers into battle. "Call your congressman, call your senators," they screamed at the top of their voices, "tell them to vote against **every proposal** put forth by the Democrats. Threaten to vote them out of office if they don't!" [Yes, they will say practically anything to exploit fear.] Speaking of fear, where was the **outrage** when President Reagan raised the tax limit 17 times? Where was the **outrage** when President Bush raised the tax limit 9 times?

Finally, the campaign to "Take Back Our Country" led to the formation of the Tea Party.

Some Suggestions for Fair and Balanced Discussions

1. Public Broadcasting, PBS, channel 13, 7pm, "News Hour"
2. Public Broadcasting, PBS, Fridays, 6pm, "Need to Know"
3. NY1, 7pm, repeated at 10pm, Errol Lewis, "Inside City Hall"
4. NY1, 9pm, "The Call," Call-in, email, and Twitter

5. WNYC, "It's a Free Country.com." Participate, read, argue, act.
6. WNYC with National Public Radio (NPR) AM 820 - 24 hours. Brian Lehrer 10am, repeated at 10pm.
7. Sunday morning talk shows. Guests, all political parties.
8. WWRL-AM 1600. Mark Riley, guests and Call-in.
9. WWRL-AM 1600. Bev. Smith, 10pm-12am. Guests and Call-in.
10. WWRL-AM 1600. Leslie Marshall, 12am-6am, Guests and Call-in.

<u>*Can't Find a Group? Become an Independent Volunteer*</u>

Obtain Voter Registration Applications from the Board of Elections at:
126-06 Queens Blvd., Kew Gardens, 718-730-6730, or 1-866-VOTENYC

Distribute to new high school graduates, new citizens, people with a name change, new address, on your job, on your block, your church, and in your building.

Support President Obama and the Democratic Party
www.obamaforamerica.com Discover what it's about!

GOD BLESS AMERICA!
By M. E. Thomas

APPENDIX 4

National, State & Local Elected Offices

National, State & Local Elected Offices

NATIONAL

Congress
U.S. Senate

↓

STATE ——→ PRESIDENT ←—— STATE

NYS Comptroller
NYS Senators
State Assembly Representatives

NYS Gover:
NYS Lt. Gover:
Public Advoc
District Attorı

↑

NYC Mayor
Borough President
NYC Comptroller
NYC Council Representatives

CITY

"We the People" Will Determine Which Laws
Are Passed or Defeated
The Majority Vote Wins!

Rosenwald Schools; available from http:// scrambleschool.org/ Rosenwaldschool.htm.

2 *Conference of The Queens Association for the Education of the Exceptionally Gifted Child, Inc.* Community School District 29, Intermediate School, Vol. 1, (New York Department of Teacher Preparation, York College of CUNY, Spring, 1973, p. 1

3 Ibid.

4 Chuck Pishko, "Remembrance of Transfer Day," St. John Tradewinds, March 17-23, 2014, p. 19.

5 Judi, Shimel. "Historic Warehouse gets new life at Maho Bay," St. John Tradewinds, March 31-April 6, 2014, pp 5 and 22.

6 Tom Oates, telephone conversation with St. John Tradewinds columnist and former editor, June 11, 2014.

7 John Barry, *Rising Tide:The Great Mississippi Flood of 1927 and How It Changed America*, 1st Touchstone ed. (New York: Simon and Schuster, 1998).

8 Jeff Biggers, *Reckoning At Eagle Creek – The Secret Legacy of Coal in the Heartland* (New York: Nation Booker, a member of the Perseus Book Group, 2010).

[9]   Mining in South Africa. Available from http;//en.wikipedia.orga/ wiki/mining-industry-of-South-Africa.

[10] Mining in Utah. Available from http://en.lwikipedia.org/wiki/ Bingham-Canyon-mine.

[11] Catherine "Cathy" Hughes. Available from_http://pinewoodw. org/about/boardmem.asp.

[12] "New Zealand's Volcanic Plateau and Rotovua, The Regional Capital," p. 2

[13] Douglas Summers Brown, ed., "The Negro in Greensville County," *Sketches of Greensville County_1650-1967* (Emporia, Virginia: Sponsored by The Riparian Woman's Club, 1968) p. 131.

[14] Bridgetta C. Jenkins, Library of Congress, U.S. Monograph Section, U.S./Anglo Division, Nov. 13, 2013.

Made in the USA
Middletown, DE
07 January 2016